"FOR A BREVET (

All U.S. Regular Army C
Indian Wars West of the Mississippi
1866-1898

By
Paul G. English

US Army Indian Wars Campaign Medal

DEDICATION
In memory of my parents.

Published By
The
Virtual
Armchair
General

Patrick R. Wilson, Editor-In-Chief

"For A Brevet Or A Coffin!"
By Paul G. English

Layout, Covers, Editing, by Patrick R. Wilson
Copyright © 2013 by The (Virtual) Armchair General
10208 Haverhill Place, Oklahoma City, OK 73120-3922 USA
Voice/Fax: (405) 752-2420
For other products and publications, visit
www.thevirtualarmchairgeneral.com
Please address questions to **TVAG@att.net**
First Printing: December, 2013
The photo of the Author appearing on the cover is courtesy of
Ms. Janna Rowe.

Cover and Frontispiece art by Charles Schreyvogel

Contents

INTRODUCTION

The 25 years after the American Civil War witnessed a full-blown effort to complete the settlement of the frontier west of the Mississippi. The gradual development of the transcontinental railroad and telegraph systems sped up this process. That the original native inhabitants already occupied these lands was seen as an annoying inconvenience by a government and people who, as a whole, manifested little sympathy and less understanding for the Indians' rights and their terrible dilemma.

There were genuine exceptions to the country's overall indifference. These included some principled Indian Agents, most notably Quakers appointed during the Grant Administration (1869-1877). For the most part, these Christian agents treated their Native charges with respect and compassion. There were also prominent Eastern humanitarians who steadily pressed the government for better treatment of the Indians.

The United States Army's unenviable and difficult task was to ensure that White settlement be accomplished in comparative safety and with minimal interference. This meant confronting the Native Americans who were in the way, subjugating them when necessary, then placing them on government reservations and working with Indian Agents to keep them there.

The Indian Wars era Army was an all volunteer force enlisted from the lowest ranks of society, men who simply could not "make it" in civilian life. Private soldiers were paid about what a skilled laborer might earn, but the harsh conditions, poor food, isolation on the frontier, and minimal chances of promotion fed desertion rates of to 25% each year, and most Cavalry and Infantry companies were woefully under strength. But there was no lack of men willing to lead them.

The following brief work is a record of the Regular Army officers killed by Indians between 1866 and 1898. Since most of the combat was at the small unit level, only a few of those killed were field-grade officers, i.e. Majors and above. Company-grade officers (Lieutenants and Captains) saw the most service and, consequently, suffered the greater loss.

The term "brevet" appearing in the title was a key feature in the US Army before the modernizations of the early 20th Century. When the Old Army of the 19th Century was strictly professional, and purposefully small, with only a finite set of officer ranks (with numbers actually limited by Congress), promotion was slow to virtually non-existent. A Lieutenant posted for active duty in the West in 1870 could hold the same rank in 1890.

During the Civil War, with the enormous number of Volunteer units and their officers in the Union Army, promotion was much easier. When that war ended, numbers of experienced soldiers and officers chose to stay in the newly reestablished Regular Army, and that posed a problem.

With a once again small professional army, career officers—many of whom were West Point graduates—felt understandably threatened by the sudden influx of veteran Volunteer Army officers to the service. No Regular Colonel, for instance, wanted to be outranked by a Volunteer General, so the "brevet" rank came even further into play.

Large numbers of Regular and former Volunteer officers, especially those of senior ranks, were backed down one or more steps to their new "official" ranks to fill those positions then existing. Thus, for example, signal war hero George A. Custer, originally a West Point 2nd Lieutenant graduate, but who accepted promotion to Major General of Volunteers, suddenly found himself a Lt. Colonel after the war. Such "adjustments" to the rolls were a bitter pill for many, but it was sugar coated, at least.

Those officers who were reduced from earlier, loftier titles, were permitted to carry their former ranks as honorifics and forms of address. Though a 10 year veteran Lieutenant, he might still be addressed as "Major." When at table among his fellow officers, he could expect to be seated by his brevet rank, rather than by that on his shoulders. In certain circumstances, one's brevet rank could make a man temporarily senior to another officer with an "official" rank

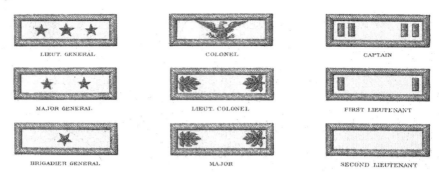

LIEUT. GENERAL.	COLONEL	CAPTAIN
MAJOR GENERAL.	LIEUT. COLONEL	FIRST LIEUTENANT
BRIGADIER GENERAL	MAJOR	SECOND LIEUTENANT

Officer rank insignia in the era of the Indian Wars

higher than his. And if actual promotion, or a plumb assignment, was a prospect, the number and/or rank of Brevets could influence who would receive it.

Further, the undersized army was often divided and subdivided into posts and garrisons over the expanding Western frontier, requiring officers of suitable rank where not enough existed, in which case brevet ranks could be granted to junior officers for such assignments.

And as promotion proved to remain as slow as ever, brevet ranks could be, but not necessarily, awarded to officers who gave exceptional service in the field.

These brought no extra pay, but, there was no better way to prove one's courage, devotion to duty, and ambition than to "earn a brevet" in the field, and many an officer pursued the succubus into the face of violent death.

Between 1866 and 1898, 68 officers and 879 enlisted men lost their lives in the trans-Mississippi Indian Wars, and more than 1,000 wounded. The total Indian combat casualties during this same period was estimated to be almost 6,000 killed and wounded. (See the *Chronological List of Actions with Indians*, pp. 23–79 and Utley, *Frontier Regulars*, p 412).

Each officer's biographical sketch which follows is headed by his name, birth date (where available), state or country of birth, rank, regiment, and branch of service at the time of death. For those graduates of the U.S. Military Academy, the date of entry is given. Many of these men saw active service in either the Regular Army or as Volunteers during the Civil War; therefore a brief war record has been provided wherever applicable.

For the sake of simplicity, all battle sites mentioned are recorded under their present state boundaries, rather than the territorial setting which many of them had at the time. Hence, the Washita River, Indian Territory, becomes the Washita River, Oklahoma.

The Congressional Medal of Honor was created in 1861 to be awarded to military personnel who performed exceptional acts of valor in combat. It was, and is, the nation's most prestigious award; many of those who have earned it have lost their lives in the process. Tom Custer, later of the 7th Cavalry, was himself awarded the medal twice during the Civil War.

Finally, the title of this work is taken from the last words of Major Joel Elliott, 7th Cavalry, overheard as he rode out of Cheyenne Chief Black Kettle's camp, during the Battle of the Washita, in pursuit of fleeing Indians. Bounding away on horseback through deep snow into frigid woods, at the head of Sgt. Major Walter Kennedy and a detachment of 17 men, Elliott cried, "Here goes for a brevet or a coffin!"

Elliott lies fallen to the left, while Sgt. Major Kennedy and his comrades experience the sanitized consequences of the former's roll of the dice.

8

ACKNOWLEDGMENTS

A number of people have assisted me in completing this project. These include my old friend Steve Stevens, who helped me with the initial research, and my great friend, Mark Megehee, Collections Manager at the Fort Sill National Historic Landmark and Museum, Fort Sill, Oklahoma, who spent an hour with me one August afternoon explaining the characteristics of the 1.65" Hotchkiss Mountain Rifle. My thanks to Museum Director Dr. Scott Neel as well as to former Museum Director Towana Spivey and Archivist Wade Popp for access to Fort Sill's museum archive.

Others who greatly assisted me include Bill Welge, Director of the Archives and Manuscript Division of the Oklahoma Historical Society in Oklahoma City, and former staff member Sharron Ashton, as well as the personnel at the Morris Swett Library at Fort Sill and the Combat Arms Research Library, Fort Leavenworth, Kansas. I am very grateful to Jan Potts of Norman, Oklahoma, for her careful preparation of the original manuscript, and Joshua Webb of

Bones on the battlefield of Little Big Horn.

Cache, Oklahoma, for providing his considerable computer skills in locating some otherwise elusive information.

Fellow Oklahomans who have helped along the way are my friends Linda Winn, Eric Cox, Suzanne Cox and Marcia Shottenkirk, as well as my former co-worker, Stephanie Opitz, who made the fine line drawing appearing on the Contents page. I also wish to thank fellow Indian Wars enthusiast, John Chadwick, U.S. Army, Ret., for his careful reading of the manuscript.

Finally, my sincere thanks to publisher Patrick Wilson of The (Virtual) Armchair General.

Paul G. English
November, 2013

US Army Infantry and Cavalry Winter Dress Uniforms, Indian Wars era.

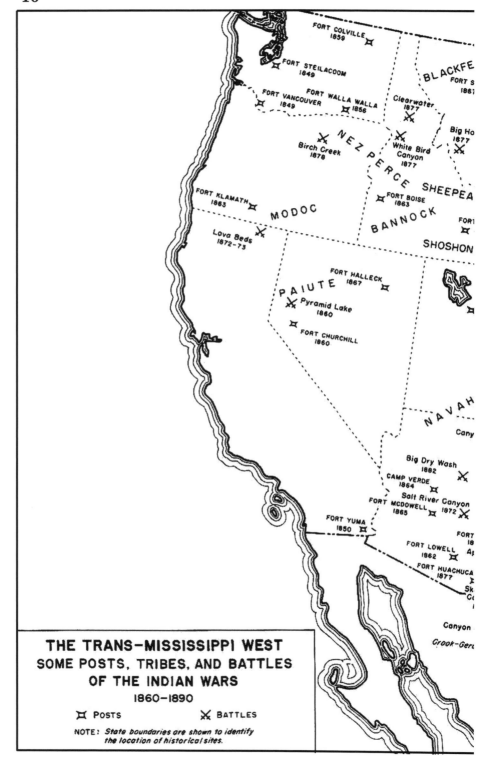

FORT COLVILLE
1859

FORT STEILACOOM
1849

BLACKFE

FORT S
1867

FORT WALLA WALLA

FORT VANCOUVER
1849

1856

Clearwater
1877

N E Z

Big Ho
1877

Birch Creek
1878

White Bird
Canyon
1877

P E R C E

SHEEPEA

FORT KLAMATH
1863

MODOC

FORT BOISE
1863

BANNOCK

FOR1

SHOSHON

Lava Beds
1872-73

FORT HALLECK
1867

P A I U T E

Pyramid Lake
1860

FORT CHURCHILL
1860

N A V A H

Cany

Big Dry Wash
1882

CAMP VERDE
1864

Salt River Canyon

FORT MCDOWELL
1865

1872

FORT YUMA
1850

FORT
18

FORT LOWELL
1862

Ap

FORT HUACHUCA
1877

Sk

C

Canyon

Crook-Ger

THE TRANS-MISSISSIPPI WEST
SOME POSTS, TRIBES, AND BATTLES
OF THE INDIAN WARS
1860–1890

Posts   Battles

NOTE: *State boundaries are shown to identify
the location of historical sites.*

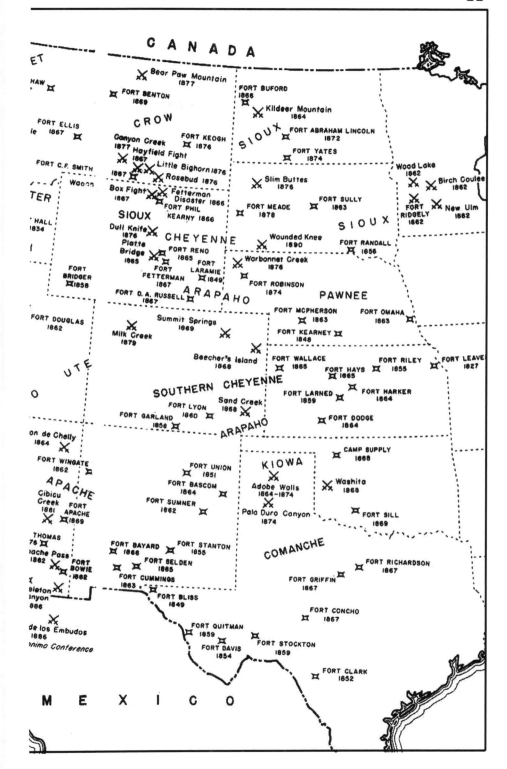

C A N A D A

Bear Paw Mountain
1877

FORT BENTON
1869

HAW

FORT BUFORD
1866

Kildeer Mountain
1864

FORT ELLIS
1867

CROW

FORT ABRAHAM LINCOLN
1872

FORT KEOGH
1876

SIOUX

Canyon Creek
1877
Hayfield Fight
1867
Little Bighorn 1876
Rosebud 1876

FORT YATES
1874

Wood Lake
1862

FORT C.F. SMITH
1867

Wagon

Slim Buttes
1876

Birch Coulee
1862

Box Fight
1867

Fetterman
Disaster 1866
FORT PHIL
KEARNY 1866

FORT MEADE
1878

FORT SULLY
1863

FORT
RIDGELY
1862

New Ulm
1862

TER

HALL
1834

SIOUX

CHEYENNE

Wounded Knee
1890

SIOUX

Dull Knife
1876
Platte
Bridge
1865

FORT RENO
1865

FORT
LARAMIE
1849

Warbonnet Creek
1876

FORT RANDALL
1856

FORT
BRIDGER
1858

FORT
FETTERMAN
1867

ARAPAHO

FORT ROBINSON
1874

PAWNEE

FORT O.A. RUSSELL
1867

FORT MCPHERSON
1863

FORT OMAHA
1863

FORT DOUGLAS
1862

UTE

Summit Springs
1869

Milk Creek
1879

FORT KEARNEY
1848

Beecher's Island
1868

FORT WALLACE
1865

FORT RILEY
1855

FORT LEAVE

SOUTHERN CHEYENNE

FORT HAYS
1865

FORT LARNED
1859

FORT HARKER
1864

FORT LYON
1860

Sand Creek
1868

FORT GARLAND
1858

ARAPAHO

FORT DODGE
1864

on de Chelly
1864

FORT WINGATE
1862

FORT UNION
1851

KIOWA

CAMP SUPPLY
1868

FORT BASCOM
1864

Adobe Walls
1864-1874

Washita
1868

APACHE

Cibicu
Creek
1881

FORT
APACHE
1869

FORT SUMNER
1862

Palo Duro Canyon
1874

FORT SILL
1869

THOMAS
76

ache Pass
1862

FORT
BOWIE
1862

FORT BAYARD
1866

FORT STANTON
1855

COMANCHE

FORT RICHARDSON
1867

FORT SELDEN
1865

eleton

nyon
866

FORT CUMMINGS
1863

FORT GRIFFIN
1867

FORT BLISS
1849

FORT CONCHO
1867

de los Embudos
1886

nimo Conference

FORT QUITMAN
1859

FORT DAVIS
1854

FORT STOCKTON
1859

FORT CLARK
1852

M E X I C O

Brief Chronology of the Indian Wars, 1866 – 1898

1866 (and before)-1886—Conflicts with the Apaches until the surrender of the bands of Geronimo and Mangus.

1866 –1868—The War with the Northern Paiutes.

1866-1868—Red Cloud's War, involving the Western (Teton) Sioux, Northern Cheyenne and Northern Arapaho's.

1867—The Medicine Lodge Treaty with the Southern Plains tribes.

1868—The Fort Laramie Treaty with the Northern Plains tribes.

1866-1873—Hostilities with the Kiowa's, Comanche's, Sioux, Southern Cheyenne, and Southern Arapaho's.

1872-1874—Hostilities with the Teton Sioux over the Northern Boundary Survey and Yellowstone Expeditions.

1872-73—The Modoc War.

1874—The Black Hills Expedition.

1874-75—The Red River War, ending with the subjugation of the hostile Southern Plains tribes (Kiowa, Comanche, Southern Cheyenne, Southern Arapaho, and Kiowa-Apache).

1876-77—The Great Sioux War.

1877—The War with the Nez Perce.

1878—The Dull Knife Episode, involving the Northern Cheyenne.

1878—The Bannock-Paiute War.

1879—The War with the Ute's.

1890-91—Last hostilities with the Sioux (Wounded Knee).

1898, October—Brief troubles with the Chippewa.

US Army Infantry and Cavalry Full Dress Uniforms during the Indian Wars era.

Alphabetical List of Officers Killed in Action

Lewis D. Adair
Ohio.
1st Lieutenant, 22nd Infantry.

Civil War Veteran, Volunteers, 1861 – 1864: Served with the 26th Ohio Infantry, attaining the rank of Captain. Honorably mustered out on 25 July 1864.

Regular Army: *Commissioned 1st Lieutenant, 22nd Infantry, on 28 July, 1866.*

On 4 October, 1872, when serving as a member of the military escort for the Northern Boundary Survey, 1st Lieutenant Adair was mortally wounded by Sioux Indians while hunting near the Heart River Crossing, North Dakota. He died the following day.

In a 1907 interview, Horn Chips, an Oglala Sioux informant, told researcher Eli S. Ricker that the Hunkpapa Sioux leader, Gall, was directly responsible for the death of Lieutenant Adair and that of 1st Lieutenant Eben Crosby a day earlier.

Jacob Almy
Born 20 November, 1842.
Massachusetts.
Entered U.S. Military Academy (U.S.M.A.) 1863.
1st Lieutenant, 5th Cavalry.

Civil War Veteran, Volunteers, 1862 – 1863: Served as a Corporal, 33rd Massachusetts Infantry. Released from the Volunteers in 1863 to enter the U.S. Military Academy.

Regular Army: *Graduated from the U.S. Military Academy and pro-*

moted to 2nd Lieutenant, 5th Cavalry, on 17 June, 1867. Promoted to 1st Lieutenant on 15 April, 1869.

Lieutenant Almy saw action with the Southern Cheyenne at Beaver and Prairie Dog Creeks, Kansas in October 1868. In July 1869, while serving as Adjutant of the Republican River Expedition, he took part in Major E. A. Carr's decisive victory over Tall Bull's Cheyenne Dog Soldiers at Summit Springs, Colorado. In 1872 – 1873, he was in action in Arizona against the Apaches at Salt River Canyon and in the Superstition Mountains.

May 27, 1873 was ration day at the San Carlos Indian Agency, Arizona. There were about 1,000 Apaches waiting for their issue of beef. First Lieutenant Almy headed the small military detachment of about 25 men assigned to the agency. Agent Larrabee, sensing serious trouble, asked Almy to arrest an Apache named Chan-deisi, who had caused problems earlier in the day.

As Almy approached a large crowd of Apaches, which included Chan-deisi, he was unarmed and alone. Suddenly, several Indians produced guns and opened fire, killing Almy almost instantly. They then fled the agency, as did nearly all the other Apaches present, though most of the Indians returned within a few days.

Over the next 14 months, the Apaches themselves, with the full support of the Army, ran Chan-deisi and his fellow renegades, Chuntz and Cochinay, to earth and accorded them the same courtesy shown Lieutenant Almy.

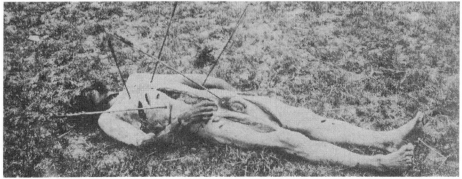

The common fate of many soldiers and civilians at the hands of Plains Indian Tribes, here lies Sgt. Frederick Wyllyams, Co. "G", 7th Cavalry, 26 June, 1867.

Frederick H. Beecher
Born 22 June, 1841. Louisiana.
1st Lieutenant, 3rd Infantry.

Civil War Veteran, Volunteers, 1862 – 1866: Served with the 16th Maine Infantry, attaining the rank of 1st Lieutenant. Resigned from active field service after being twice wounded, notably at Gettysburg where he was severely wounded in the knee by a shell fragment. Served as a 2nd Lieutenant of the Veteran Reserve Corps, 1864–1865. Honorably mustered out on 3 March, 1866.

Brevetted: *1st Lieutenant and Captain of Volunteers, on 5 December, 1865, for gallant and meritorious service during the war.*

Regular Army: *Commissioned 2nd Lieutenant, 3rd Infantry, on 29 November, 1865. Promoted to 1st Lieutenant on 28 July, 1866.*

In the wake of brutal attacks on the Kansas settlements by Cheyenne war parties, General Sheridan ordered Major G. A. Forsyth of his staff to raise a company of 50 experienced frontiersmen to work as scouts against the hostiles. Forsyth and 1st Lieutenant Beecher were to serve as the company's officers.

On the morning of 17 September, 1868, while the scouts camped on the Arickaree Fork of the Republican River in Northeastern Colorado, several hundred Cheyenne and Sioux warriors suddenly attacked. Forsyth and his men quickly entrenched themselves on a low island in the river, and held off

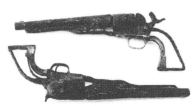

A brace of Colt Revolvers excavated from the site of Beecher's Island.

the Indians for a week until rescued on 25 September by troops from Fort Wallace, Kansas.

First Lieutenant Beecher was killed on the first day, and five others perished in the savage fight. In addition, Forsyth and several of the scouts were badly wounded but recovered. All suffered from exposure and hunger. The enemy lost the noted Southern Cheyenne War Chief, Roman Nose, and more than 30 warriors.

Sometimes called the fight on the Arickaree, the battle is best remembered as the "Beecher's Island Fight," in honor of the slain lieutenant.

Frederick Beecher was the grandson of noted abolitionist Lyman Beecher and the nephew of writer Harriet Beecher Stowe.

Andrew S. Bennett
New York.
Captain, 5th Infantry.

Civil War Veteran, Volunteers, 1861 – 1864: Served with the 5th Wisconsin Infantry, attaining the rank of 1st Lieutenant and performing the duties of Regimental Adjutant. He saw action in General G. B. McClellan's Peninsular Campaign in 1862, and in the campaigns of Antietam, Get-tysburg, and The Wilderness before being honorably mus-tered out on 2 August, 1864.

Regular Army: *Commissioned 1st Lieutenant, 15th Infan-try, on 7 March, 1867. Promoted to Captain on 28 February, 1869. Unassigned 12 August, 1869. Assigned to the 5th Infantry on 1 January,1871.*

Captain Bennett served with his regiment in the Sioux War of 1876 and in the closing days of the Nez Perce Campaign of 1877. The following year he was again on active service during the Bannock – Paiute War.

At daybreak, on 4 September, 1878, Captain Bennett was killed in an assault by mounted infantry and Crow Scouts on a Bannock Indian camp at Clark's Fork, Montana.

Jonathan W. Biddle
Pennsylvania.
2nd Lieutenant, 7th Cavalry.

Regular Army: Commissioned 2nd Lieutenant, 7th Cavalry, on 21 August 1876.

On 30 September, 1877, in the frontal assault on the Nez Perce position on Snake Creek near the Bear Paw Mountains in Northern Montana, 2nd Lieutenant Biddle and his commander, Captain Hale, were killed and their "K" Company badly mauled. The Lieutenant's body was reportedly struck several times by both army and Nez Perce bullets as it lay on the field between the opposing forces.

Horatio S. Bingham
Born 31 August, 1837. Canada.
2nd Lieutenant, 2nd Cavalry.

Civil War Veteran, Volunteers, 1863 – 1866: Served with the 2nd Minnesota Cavalry, attaining the rank of Captain. Honorably mustered out on 19 April, 1866.

Regular Army: Commissioned 2nd Lieutenant, 2nd Cavalry, on 23 February, 1866.

Some months after receiving his commission, 2nd Lieutenant Bingham was assigned to Fort Phil Kearny, Wyoming and arrived at the post on 3 November, 1866, the same day as the equally ill fated Captain W. J. Fetterman.

Fort Phil Kearny, situated in the midst of hostile Sioux and Northern Cheyenne country, was for all practical purposes in a state of siege and had been since its establishment the previous summer. Any person or parties venturing beyond the fort's stockade walls were subject to assault.

Early on the afternoon of 6 December, 1866, a wood cutting party working near the post was attacked. Infantry detachments, including Captains Fetterman and Fred Brown, and 2nd Lieutenant Bingham's "C" Company, 2nd Cavalry, all led by Colonel Carrington, the post's commander, immediately rode to engage the Indians.

In the confusion of the ensuing skirmishes, Bingham, 2nd Lieutenant Grummond, Sergeant Bowers, and several troopers rode into an ambush. Lieutenant Bingham was killed and Sergeant Bowers mortally wounded. Grummond and the others escaped but had to fight their way through a swarm of determined warriors. Lieutenant Bingham's body was recovered that evening. He had been shot in the head, scalped and struck with more than 50 arrows.

James H. Bradley
Born 25 May 1844. Ohio.
1st Lieutenant, 7th Infantry.

Civil War Veteran, Volunteers, 1861 and 1862–1865: Served with the 14th and 45th Ohio Infantry Regiments, attaining the rank of Sergeant. He participated in the early eastern battles of Philippi, Laurel Hill, and Carrick's Ford, Virginia. He was in Georgia and Tennessee later in the conflict and served in numerous engagements including Kennesaw Mountain, Peach Tree Creek, the siege of Atlanta, Jonesboro, Franklin, and Nashville. Honorably mustered out on 5 July, 1865.

Regular Army: *Commissioned 2nd Lieutenant, 18th Infantry, on 23 February, 1866. Promoted to 1st Lieutenant on 29 July, 1866. Transferred to the 7th Infantry on 28 November, 1871.*

Big Hole Battle - Gibbons. Aug.9.

While en route to Fort Phil Kearny, Wyoming, on 21 July, 1866, 2nd Lieutenant Bradley's party was engaged in a hard fight with the Sioux near the Crazy Woman's Fork of the Powder River. The fight was immediately preceded by the ambush and slaying of 1st Lieutenant Napoleon Daniels, 18th Infantry, who was hunting with a second officer some distance from the escort.

As a member of Colonel Gibbon's Montana Column, 1st Lieutenant Bradley gave untiring service as Chief of Scouts during the Sioux War of 1876. His Crow Scouts found the bodies of Custer's battalion, and he was among the troops which relieved Major Reno's beleaguered command at the Little Big Horn.

In the summer of 1877, Bradley was again on active service in the field when, on 9 August, he was killed in the 7th Infantry's desperate battle with Chief Joseph's Nez Perce at the Big Hole Basin in Southwestern Montana.

The fight at the Big Hole was among the most severe in the history of the Indian Wars. It began with Colonel John Gibbon's dawn assault on the Nez Perce encampment

Model 1873 Springfield Carbine issued to all US Cavalry Regiments, and carried by the 7th Cavalry at the Battle of Little Big Horn.

and ended with the Indians, led by Chiefs Looking Glass and White Bird, driving back the attackers and placing them in a state of siege, with the possibility of annihilation not entirely out of the question. Joseph's people broke off action on the evening of the following day, in order to continue their long retreat to the Canadian border, where they hoped to escape the pursuing army for good.

Colonel Gibbon, himself severely wounded in the thigh, lost from his command 31 killed and many wounded. The Nez Perce suffered nearly 90 killed of all ages, including a number of women, who died fighting along side their husbands and brothers.

Frederick H. Brown
New York.
Captain, 18th Infantry.

Civil War Veteran, Regular Army: Entered the army as a Private and Quartermaster Sergeant, 18th Infantry, in 1861. Commissioned 2nd Lieutenant on 30 October, 1861. Served as the Regimental Quartermaster from 4 November, 1861 until the year of his death. Promoted to 1st Lieutenant on 24 March, 1862 and to Captain, on 15 May, 1866.

Brevetted: *Captain, on 1 September, 1864, for gallant and meritorious service in the Atlanta Campaign.*

Captain Brown was assigned to Colonel Henry Carrington's command in 1866 and assisted in the establishment of Fort Phil Kearny, Wyoming, in the summer of that year. In the following months he fought the Sioux in several skirmishes near the post.

An old friend of Captain W. J. Fetterman, 27th Infantry, with whom he had served in the late Civil War,

Brown supported him in promoting a more aggressive policy toward the Indians.

Late on the morning of 21 December, 1866, Captain Fetterman was assigned to relieve a wood train under attack by the Sioux. Wanting to see one last action before his transfer to Fort Laramie for reassignment, Captain Brown obtained consent from the post commander to join his friend and died with him when the whole command was overwhelmed and annihilated by the Indians an hour later.

His body, riddled with more than 100 arrows, was recovered that evening.

James Calhoun
Born 24 August 1845. Ohio.
1st Lieutenant, 7th Cavalry.

Regular Army: *Entered the army as a Private, 14th Infantry in 1864. Having attained the rank of Sergeant, he transferred to the 32nd Infantry on 31 July, 1867 and was commissioned a 2nd Lieutenant. On 19 April, 1869, he transferred to the 21st Infantry, when the 32nd was combined with the 21st. Temporarily unassigned in 1870, he was next assigned to the 7th Cavalry, and promoted to 1st Lieutenant, on 9 January, 1871.*

US 7th Cavalry cap insignia style authorized at the time of Little Big Horn.

First Lieutenant Calhoun married Margaret, sister of Lieutenant Colonel G. A. Custer, in 1872. He served as Custer's Adjutant on both the Yellowstone and Black Hills Expeditions in 1873 and 1874.

On 25 June, 1876, while commanding "L" Company of the Custer Battalion, he was killed in action with Sioux and Northern Cheyenne warriors at the Little Big Horn River, Montana.

The positions of the bodies and expended cartridges found around them indicated that Calhoun and his company of approximately 40 men had resolutely stood their ground, until completely overwhelmed.

Edward R. S. Canby
Born 9 November 1817. Kentucky.
Entered U.S.M.A 1835.
Brigadier General, U.S. Army.

Regular Army: Graduated from the U.S. Military Academy and promoted to 2nd Lieutenant, 2nd Infantry, on 1 July, 1839. Served with his regiment in the Second Seminole War. He was the Regimental Adjutant from 24 March, 1846, to 3 March, 1847. Promoted to 1st Lieutenant on 18 June, 1846. He saw action with General Winfield Scott's army in the Mexican War in 1847. Promoted to Major, 10th Infantry, on 3 March, 1855. Served under Colonel Albert Sidney Johnston in the Mormon Expedition of 1857–1858. Promoted to Colonel, 19th Infantry, 14 May, 1861.

In the opening year of the Civil War, he commanded the Union forces in the Southwest and successfully stopped Confederate General Sibley's advance at the battles of Apache Canyon and Glorieta Pass, New Mexico, in March, 1862. He was appointed Brigadier General of Volunteers on 31 March of that year and made an Assistant Adjutant General in the War Department. On 7 May, 1864, he was promoted to Major General of Volunteers in command of the Division of West Mississippi.

General Canby's troops coordinated with Admiral Farragut's naval forces in the successful reduction of Mobile, Alabama, in the spring of 1865. In May he received the surrenders of the armies of Generals Richard Taylor and Kirby Smith, the last major Confederate forces in the field. He was honorably mustered out of the Volunteers on 1 September, 1866.

Mexican War Brevets: *Brevetted Captain and Assistant Adjutant General on 3 March, 1847. Brevetted Major, on 20 August, 1847, for gallant and meritorious conduct at Contreras and Churubusco, Mexico. Brevetted Lieutenant Colonel, on 13 September, 1847, for gallant conduct in the action at the Belen Gate of Mexico City.*

Civil War Brevets: *Brevetted Brigadier General and Major General respectively, retroactive to 13 March, 1865, for gallant and meritorious service at Valverde, New Mexico and in the capture of Fort Blakely and Mobile, Alabama.*

Post-War Service: *Promoted to Brigadier General, U.S. Army, on 28 July 1866. After the war, General Canby commanded in three of the five military districts established to bring reconstruction to the war-torn South. Here he was well respected for his tact, fairness and administrative abilities. In 1870 General Canby was given command of the Department of the Columbia in the Northwest.*

In November 1872, war broke out between the Whites and warlike Modoc Indians of Northern California. After months of costly and ineffective fighting between the army and the Indians, General Canby came to the Modoc stronghold in the remote Lava Beds in an attempt to work out a peaceful settlement of the hostilities.

On 11 April, 1873, General Canby, Reverend Eleasar Thomas, a Methodist minister, and two other civilian commissioners met with the Modoc leader, Captain Jack, and several of his men in what was intended to be a peace conference. Two of the commissioners carried concealed derringers, but Canby and the minister were unarmed.

Contemporary popular press representation of General Canby's murder at the hands of the Modocs.

Suddenly, the Modocs produced weapons and opened fire on Canby's party. The General and Reverend Thomas died immediately, and the other two barely escaped.

A few months after this treachery, the Modocs were finally beaten, and in October Captain Jack and two others were tried and hanged for their part in the murders.

General Canby has the distinction of being one of only two U.S. Regular Army Generals to be killed by Indians. The first was Major General Richard Butler who was killed by Miami's or their allies in the St. Clair Disaster near the site of Fort Recovery, Ohio, on 4 November 1791. (See Heitman, *Historical Register, Vol. I*, p. 270 and Johnson, *Dictionary of American Biography, Vol. 3*, p. 366).

John C. Carroll
Kentucky.
1st Lieutenant, 32nd Infantry.

Civil War Veteran, Volunteers, 1861 – 1865: Served with the 15th Kentucky Infantry, attaining the rank of Captain. Honorably mustered out on 14 January, 1865.

Regular Army: *Commissioned 2nd Lieutenant, 14th Infantry, on 23 February, 1866 and promoted to 1st Lieutenant on the same day. Transferred to the 32nd Infantry on 21 September, 1866.*

On 5 November, 1867, while attempting to recover cattle stolen by Indians near Fort Bowie, Arizona, 1st

Lieutenant Carroll and a civilian employee were ambushed and killed by Apaches a few miles west of the post.

Edward W. Casey

Born 1 December 1850.
California.
Entered U.S.M.A. 1869.
1st Lieutenant, 22nd Infantry.

Regular Army: *Graduated from the U.S. Military Academy and promoted to 2nd Lieutenant, 22nd Infantry, on 13 June, 1873. Promoted to 1st Lieutenant on 11 January, 1880. Served with the Montana Column under Colonel Gibbon in the Sioux War of 1876. In the following year, under Colonel N.A. Miles' command, he saw action against the Sioux at Wolf Mountain and at Muddy Creek, Montana, where he led a charge. In active service against the Ute's in Colorado in 1879 – 1880. Taught tactics at the U.S. Military Academy from 1880 to 1884. Served as Regimental Adjutant of the 22nd Infantry, 1884 – 1887.*

Brevetted: *1st Lieutenant on 27 February, 1890, retroactive to 7 May, 1877, for gallant service in action against Sioux Indians at Muddy Creek, Montana.*

In June 1888, 1st Lieutenant Casey was named to command the Cheyenne Scouts at Fort Keogh, Montana, and soon became one of the most respected commanders of

M 1873 Winchester Rifle, commonly used by Plains and Southwest Indians as well as advancing White Settlers, but not by the US Army. Significant numbers of these and Henry Rifles in Indian hands would play a pivotal part at Little Bighorn.

Indian Scouts in the army.

On 7 January, 1891, near the Pine Ridge Agency, South Dakota, 1st Lieutenant Casey was shot through the head by Plenty Horses, a Brulé Sioux warrior. The young Indian killed the officer to demonstrate the unity he felt with his people and because he wished to be a martyr for their cause.

Initially, Plenty Horses was arrested for murder. Casey had, after all, been shot from behind without provocation. After weighing the matter however, a Federal Court determined that the officer's death was technically not murder but rather a hostile act committed during a time of war. When it is recalled that Lieutenant Casey's death occurred only ten days after the Wounded Knee disaster, where many Sioux had needlessly died, the Court's decision was both fair and reasonable. (See George Wallace, pg. 77). The young warrior was therefore released and the matter dropped.

William W. Cooke
Born 29 May 1846. Canada.
1st Lieutenant, 7th Cavalry.

Civil War Veteran, Volunteers, 1864 – 1865: Served with the 24th New York Cavalry, attaining the rank of 1st Lieutenant. Honorably mustered out of the Volunteers on 25 June 1865.

Regular Army: *Commissioned 2nd Lieutenant, 7th Cavalry, on 28 July 1866. Promoted to 1st Lieutenant on 31 July 1867. Served as Regimental Adjutant, 1866 – 1867 and from 1 January, 1871 until his death.*

Brevetted: *Captain, Major and Lieutenant Colonel respectively, on 2 March, 1867, for gallant and meritorious service in the battles of Petersburg, Dinwiddie Court House and Sayler's Creek, Virginia.*

Lieutenant Cooke served in General Hancock's 1867 Campaign against the Southern Cheyenne and their Sioux allies where, in command of a supply train, he fought a protracted battle with the hostiles. In November 1868, he commanded a company of 40 handpicked men, called "Cooke's Sharpshooters," in Custer's attack on Black Kettle's camp of Southern Cheyenne on the Washita River in Western Oklahoma.

As Regimental Adjutant, Cooke was with the Custer Battalion at the Little Big Horn on 25 June, 1876. As Custer approached Sitting Bull's gigantic encampment that afternoon, Adjutant Cooke sent scribbled messages by several couriers to Captain Benteen, some miles distant, to hurry that officer's battalion forward to support Custer. The last, sent with Trumpeter John Martin, read:

> *"Benteen. Come on. Big village. Be quick. Bring [ammunition] packs. P.S. Bring pacs [sic] [signed] W. W. Cooke."* [2]

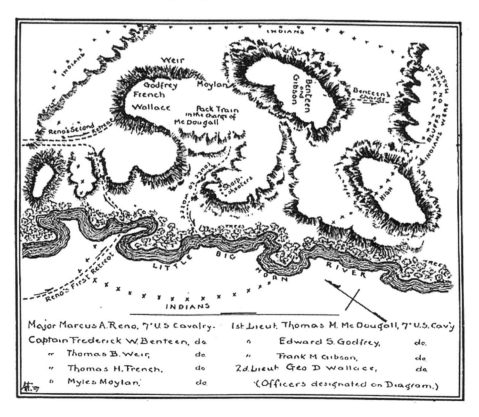

Major Marcus A. Reno, 7° U.S Cavalry.   1st Lieut. Thomas M. McDougall, 7° U.S. Cav'y
Captain Frederick W. Benteen, do.   " Edward S. Godfrey,   do.
    " Thomas B. Weir,   do.   " Frank M. Gibson,   do.
    " Thomas H. French,   do.   2d. Lieut Geo D Wallace,   do.
    " Myles Moylan,   do.   (Officers designated on Diagram.)

A short time later, Lieutenant Cooke died with Custer's entire battalion in action with the numerically superior Indian force. According to one Cheyenne participant, the fight lasted but 20 minutes. (See Stewart, *Custer's Luck*, p. 458).

Arthur Cranston

Born c. 1842/43. Massachusetts.
Entered U.S.M.A. 1862.
1st Lieutenant, 4th Artillery.

Civil War Veteran, Volunteers, 1861 – 1862: Served with the 7th and 55th Ohio Infantry Regiments, attaining the rank of 2nd Lieutenant. Resigned 15 March, 1862 to enter the U.S. Military Academy.

Regular Army: *Graduated from the U.S. Military Academy and promoted to 2nd Lieutenant, 4th Artillery, on 17 June, 1867. Promoted to 1st Lieutenant on 30 November, 1871.*

First Lieutenant Cranston was killed on 26 April, 1873, in action with Modoc Indians, in the ambush remembered as the Thomas-Wright Massacre in the Lava Beds, Northern California. (See Evan Thomas, p. 73).

Early model Henry Rifle used experimentally by the US. Army during and shortly after the Civil War, but eventually rejected in favor of the single shot Springfield Carbine with its greater range and stopping power. However, the Henry's 16 shot capacity proved to be a quantity with a quality of its own in the hands of Civilians, Scouts, Plains and Southwest Indians alike.

Emmet Crawford

Born 6 September 1844.
Pennsylvania.
Captain, 3rd Cavalry.

Civil War Veteran, Volunteers and Regular Army, 1861 – 1865: Served with the 71st and 197th Pennsylvania Infantry Regiments, attaining the rank of 1st Sergeant. He saw active service with the Army of the Potomac from York-town to the Wilderness. Commissioned 1st Lieutenant, 13th U.S. Colored Infantry, Regular Army, on 23 November, 1864. Honorably mustered out on 18 November, 1865.

Brevetted: *Captain and Major of Volunteers, on 13 March, 1865, for meritorious service during the War.*

Post-War Regular Army:
Re-entered the army as a 2nd Lieutenant, 37th U.S. Colored Infantry, on 16 February, 1866. Mustered out of the 37th U.S.C.I. on 19 May, 1867. Commissioned 2nd Lieutenant, 39th Infantry, to rank from 22 January, 1867. Promoted to 1st Lieutenant on 5 June, 1868. Transferred to the 25th Infantry on 20 April, 1869. Unassigned from 17 June, 1869. Assigned to the 3rd Cavalry on 1 January, 1871. Promoted to Captain on 20 March, 1879.

One of General George Crook's most trusted officers, Captain Crawford served under him in Arizona in campaigns against the Apaches in the 1870s and 1880s. As a company commander in the Sioux War of 1876, he participated in the fights at the Rosebud River, Montana, on 17 June, 1876, and at Slim Buttes, South Dakota, the following September.

On 11 January, 1886, Captain Crawford was mortally wounded by a Tarahumara Indian scout for the Mexican Army near Nacori, Mexico. As the Captain was engaged in a parley with the Mexicans and attempting to avert trouble, the shooting appears to have been entirely unprovoked.

Shot through the head, Captain Crawford never regained consciousness and succumbed to his wound on 18 January, 1886.

John J. Crittenden
Born 7 June 1854. Kentucky.
2nd Lieutenant, 20th Infantry.

Regular Army: Commissioned
2nd Lieutenant, 20th Infantry, on
15 October, 1875.

The son of Colonel Thomas L. Crittenden, 17th Infantry, Lieutenant Crittenden lost an eye when a shotgun accidently discharged in his face only ten days after receiving his commission. After returning from convalescent leave, he was attached for temporary duty to the 7th Cavalry.

On 25 June, 1876, while acting as Executive Officer of "L" Company, the Custer Battalion, 2nd Lieutenant Crittenden was killed in action at the Little Big Horn River, Montana. When found two days later, his body was described as having "numerous arrows sticking in it."[3] His remains were positively identified by his shattered glass eye which had been struck by an arrow.

The youngest officer lost at the Little Big Horn, his remains were interred at the battle site until 1931, when they were removed to the nearby Custer Battlefield National Cemetery. This was in keeping with the request of his father, who stated simply, "Let my boy lie where he fell."[4]

Colt Model 1873 Single Action Army Pistol as carried by US Cavalry at the time of the Little Big Horn fight.

Eben Crosby
Maine.
1st Lieutenant, 17th Infantry.

Civil War Veteran, Volunteers, 1861 – 1866: Served with the 6th Maine Infantry to 1864, attaining the rank of 1st Sergeant. Commissioned 2nd Lieutenant, Veteran Reserve Corps, on 30 March, 1864. Honorably mustered out on 30 June, 1866.

Regular Army: Commissioned 2nd Lieutenant, 44th Infantry, on 28 July, 1866. Transferred to the 17th Infantry on 27 May, 1869. Promoted to 1st Lieutenant on 30, June, 1872.

On 3 October, 1872, 1st Lieutenant Crosby, serving as a member of the military escort for the Northern Boundary Survey, was hunting near the Heart River Crossing, North Dakota, when he was killed by Sioux Indians. The following day the same fate befell 1st Lieutenant Adair, 22nd Infantry.

Howard B. Cushing
Born 22 August 1838. Wisconsin.
1st Lieutenant, 3rd Cavalry.

Civil War Veteran, Volunteers and Regular Army, 1862 – 1865: Entered the Volunteers in 1862 as a Private, 1st Illinois Artillery. Commissioned 2nd Lieutenant, 4th U.S. Artillery, on 30 November, 1863.

Post-War Regular Army:
Transferred to the 3rd Cavalry on 7 September, 1867. Promoted to 1st Lieutenant on 16 December, 1867.

LIEUTENANT HOWARD B. CUSHING

The brother of 1st Lieutenant Alonzo Cushing, 4th

Artillery, who died at Gettysburg bravely defending his battery, 1st Lieutenant Cushing distinguished himself in several Apache campaigns in West Texas, New Mexico and Arizona during his short but admirable career as an Indian fighter. A relentless opponent, he was in a dozen actions between November 1869 and the spring of 1871.

On 5 May 1871, while engaged in a heated skirmish with Chiracahua Apaches in Arizona's Whetstone Mountains, Lieutenant Cushing was wounded in the chest. His comrades were attempting to move him to safety when he was struck by a second shot through the head.

George A. Custer

Born 5 December, 1839. Ohio.
Entered U.S.M.A. 1857.
Lieutenant Colonel, 7th Cavalry.

Civil War Veteran, Regular Army and Volunteers, 1861 – 1866: Graduated from the U.S. Military Academy and promoted to 2nd Lieutenant, 2nd Cavalry, on 24 June, 1861. Transferred to the 5th Cavalry on 3 August,1861. Promoted to 1st Lieutenant on 17 July 1862. Served as Captain, aide-de-camp to Major General G.B. McClellan in 1862 and as aide-de-camp to General Pleasanton in 1863. Promoted to Captain, 5th Cavalry, on 8 May 1864. Commissioned a Brigadier General of Volunteers on 29 June, 1863 and Major General of Volunteers on 15 April, 1865.

Participated in numerous skirmishes, battles and campaigns of the Army of the Potomac including: First Bull Run, the Peninsula, South Mountain, Antietam, Brandy Station, Gettysburg, the Wilderness, Todd's Tavern, Yellow Tavern, Meadow Bridge, Hawe's Shop, Cold Harbor, Trevillian Station, Fisher's Hill, Winchester, Cedar Creek, Dinwiddie Courthouse, Five Forks, Sayler's Creek, and Appomattox.

Honorably mustered out of the Volunteers on 1 February, 1866, with the rank of Major General.

Brevetted Major on 3 July, 1863, for gallant and meritorious service at Gettysburg, Pennsylvania. Brevetted Lieutenant Colonel on 11 May, 1864, for service at Yellow Tavern, Virginia. Brevetted Colonel on 19 September, 1864, for service at Winchester, Virginia. Brevetted Brigadier and Major General respectively, retroactive to 13 March, 1865, for services at Five Forks, Virginia and for the campaign ending with the surrender of the Army of Northern Virginia. Brevetted Major General of Volunteers on 19 October, 1864, for gallant and meritorious services at Winchester and Fisher's Hill, Virginia.

Post-War Regular Army: *Having returned to his regular rank of Captain with the war's end, he was, on 28 July, 1866, promoted to Lieutenant Colonel of the newly formed 7th Cavalry.*

Lieutenant Colonel Custer and his regiment were

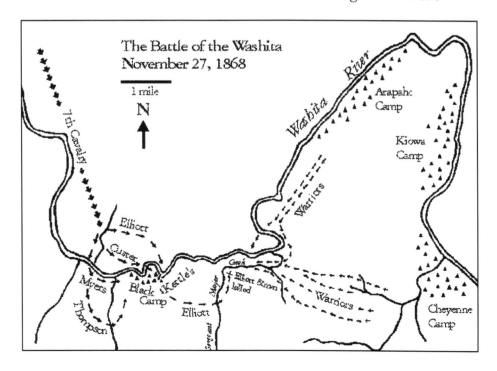

actively engaged in General W.S. Hancock's 1867 Campaign against the Southern Cheyenne and their Sioux allies. He was court-martialed and suspended from duty during this period, for leaving his command to visit his wife at Fort Riley, Kansas and for his harsh treatment of deserters. His excellent reputation as a competent field officer led to his reinstatement within the year.

In Major General P.H. Sheridan's 1868 Campaign against the hostile Southern Plains tribes, Custer commanded the successful dawn assault of his regiment on Black Kettle's encampment of Southern Cheyenne at the Washita River in Western Oklahoma.

Lieutenant Colonel Custer served in the Yellowstone Expedition of 1873, where troops of the 7th were successfully engaged in fights with the Sioux on the Tongue River, Montana, on 4 August and on the Yellowstone River, Montana, on 11 August, 1873.

In 1874 Lieutenant Colonel Custer led his regiment in the survey expedition to the Black Hills, South Dakota. The finding of gold in this region, most sacred to the Sioux, was a contributing factor to the war with them in 1876.

In the late spring of 1876 the 7th, led by Custer, served as the scouting regiment for General Alfred Terry's Expedition against the Sioux. On 25 June, Custer located Sitting Bull's huge encampment on the Little Big Horn River in Southeastern Montana. Refusing to believe his Crow and Arikara Scouts' assessment of the numerical strength of the enemy, he unwisely separated his command of 647 men into three small and widely spaced battalions, with troops detached to protect the regiment's vulnerable supply train, in a futile attempt to block the Indians' escape.

A few hours later, the battalion of five companies under his own command, numbering but 206 men, was overwhelmed and completely annihilated in a juggernaut assault of possibly 1500 warriors. Their principal leaders were Crazy Horse, Gall and Crow King of the Sioux, and Two Moon of the Northern Cheyenne. (See Gray, *Centennial Campaign*, pp. 346–357 and Stewart, *Custer's Luck*, pp. 309-312 for controversy on number of warriors involved).

About four miles distant from Custer's force, Major Reno's battalion, though badly beaten with the loss of nearly half its strength, managed to unite with that of Captain Benteen and the men of the regiment's supply train. Together, they entrenched themselves on a hilltop and held out against the Indians, until General Terry's troops arrived to rescue them two days later. It was only then that they learned of the fate of the Custer Battalion.

With 263 dead, the Little Big Horn was, by far, the army's costliest fight west of the Mississippi. By comparison, according to most Indian informants, the Sioux and Cheyenne, while suffering many wounded, lost only about 30 warriors killed or mortally wounded. Among the dead was Flying Charge, son of the prominent Hunkpapa Chief Black Moon, and a respected Cheyenne leader named Lame White Man. (See Hardorff, *Hokahey!* pp. 121-155 for extensive analysis of Indian casualties at the Little Big Horn).

George A. Custer was a colorful and flamboyant figure with a tremendous popular appeal. In the face of great odds, he always exhibited the most determined audacity which, combined with the luck that often favors the bold, had carried him triumphant through a hundred battles and skirmishes. This "Custer's Luck," in which he placed so much store, finally ran out in his last and best known fight.

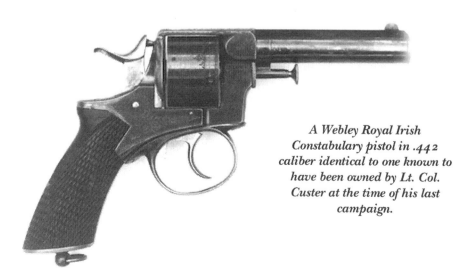

A Webley Royal Irish Constabulary pistol in .442 caliber identical to one known to have been owned by Lt. Col. Custer at the time of his last campaign.

Thomas W. Custer
Born 15 March, 1845. Ohio.
Captain, 7th Cavalry.

Civil War Veteran, Volunteers, 1861 – 1865: Served with the 21st Ohio Infantry and the 6th Michigan Cavalry, attaining the rank of 2nd Lieutenant. Before transferring to the Eastern Theater in November 1864 to serve as aide-de-camp to his brother, Major General G. A. Custer, he participated in a number of engagements in the west including Stone's River, Chickamauga, Missionary Ridge, Kennesaw Mountain, the siege of Atlanta, and Jonesboro. Honorably mustered out on 24 November, 1865.*

Brevetted First Lieutenant, Captain and Major of Volunteers, on 13 March, 1865, for distinguished and gallant conduct during the War.

The Congressional Medal of Honor

Awards: *Twice awarded the Congressional Medal of Honor on 24 April, and 22 May, 1865 for the capture of battle flags at Namozine Church and Sayler's Creek, Virginia.*

Regular Army: *Commissioned 2nd Lieutenant, 1st Infantry, on 23 February, 1866. Transferred to the 7th Cavalry, with promotion to 1st Lieutenant, on 28 July, 1866. Served as Regimental Quartermaster, 1866 – 1867. Promoted to Captain on 2 December, 1875.*

Brevetted Captain, Major and Lieutenant Colonel, on 2 March, 1867, for gallant and distinguished conduct at

Waynesboro, Virginia and near Namozine Church, Virginia, and for distinguished courage and service at Sayler's Creek, Virginia.

He served with his regiment in Hancock's 1867 Campaign against the Southern Cheyenne and their allies, in his brother's fight on the Washita in November 1868 and in the 7th's two engagements with the Sioux on the Tongue and Yellowstone Rivers in August 1873.

Captain Custer met his death while commanding "C" Company, the Custer Battalion, on the field of the Little Big Horn, on 25 June, 1876. His body was horribly mutilated – scalped, decapitated and disemboweled.

Napoleon H. Daniels
Louisiana.
1st Lieutenant, 18th Infantry.

Civil War Veteran, Volunteers, 1861 – 1865: Attained the rank of 1st Lieutenant, 18th Indiana Infantry. Honorably mustered out on 28 August, 1865.

Regular Army: *Commissioned 2nd Lieutenant and promoted to 1st Lieutenant, 18th Infantry, on 23 February, 1866.*

On 21 July, 1866, when en route to Fort Phil Kearny, Wyoming, 1st Lieutenant Daniels and a fellow officer were ambushed by Sioux Indians, while hunting near the Crazy Woman's Fork of the Powder River. Though wounded, Daniels' companion managed to escape. The Lieutenant's body, bristling with 22 arrows, was recovered the following day.

Afterwards, a witness reported that Daniels had been very troubled by thoughts of impending death the night before he was killed.

Joel H. Elliott

Born 27 October, 1840. Indiana.
Major, 7th Cavalry.

Civil War Veteran, Volunteers, 1861 – 1866: Served with the 2nd and 7th Indiana Cavalry Regiments in the Western Theater. Elliott fought at Shiloh, Perryville, Stone's River, and Corinth. For distinguishing himself in the battle of Perryville, Kentucky in October of 1862, he received a commission in June of the following year. In the fall of 1863, he was promoted to Captain. On 10 June, 1864, he was very seriously wounded in the left lung during the engagement at Brice's Cross Roads, Mississippi but was able to return to active duty the following January. Honorably mustered out of the Volunteers on 18 February, 1866.

Regular Army: Having scored very high on the officer's entrance examination and with the thorough approval of such high ranking soldiers as Lieutenant Colonel G.A. Custer, who considered him a "natural soldier[5]," Elliott entered the Regular Army on 7 March, 1867 with the high rank of Major, 7th Cavalry.

Major Elliott was with his regiment in General Hancock's Campaign against the Southern Cheyenne and their allies in 1867, and he commanded the military escort for the Medicine Lodge Treaty proceedings in Kansas in the fall of that year. In September of 1868, during Custer's absence, he commanded the 7th Cavalry in Sully's Expedition against the Kiowa's and Comanche's.

On 27 November, 1868, Major Elliott led one of Lieutenant Colonel Custer's assault columns in the dawn attack on Black Kettle's camp of Southern Cheyenne on the Washita River in Western Oklahoma.

THE SEVENTH U.S. CAVALRY CHARGING INTO BLACK KETTLE'S VILLAGE AT DAYLIGHT, November 27, 1868.—[SEE PAGE 811.]

In the midst of the battle, Major Elliott, with 18 soldiers, pursued several fleeing Indians down the river with the intent of capturing them. The Major soon found himself surrounded by Kiowa, Comanche, Cheyenne, and Arapaho warriors coming from undetected camps further downstream to assist Black Kettle's people. Elliott ordered his men to dismount and take cover in some tall grass. The Indians were able to get in positions above them, however, and all were killed in a few minutes.

After the battle Custer made no serious attempt to look for the missing Major. Though he had a full regiment at his disposal, he was now confronted by an unknown number of warriors from the nearby camps who might attack at any moment. Custer was not normally one to be particularly concerned by a numerous enemy, but he had accomplished his mission. In addition to this, his men were exhausted and some were wounded.

At any rate, Custer had no idea where Elliott was or even if he was still alive, so he elected to break off action and march his men off the battlefield. The Indians made some feints toward his column and fired from a distance but did not pursue. Whatever Custer's reasons were for his decision not to conduct a thorough search, he was roundly criticized later by some of his fellow officers, including General Sheridan himself, for his failure to do so. The frozen, badly mutilated bodies of Elliott and his men were located and buried two weeks later.

In his post-battle report, Custer stated that his regiment had killed 103 warriors, captured 53 prisoners and destroyed almost 900 war ponies and the entire Indian camp. Other sources from the same period reckon as actually killed, somewhere between 9 and 20 fighting men and between 18 and 40 women and children (see Berthrong, *The Southern Cheyenne*, p 328).

The most noteworthy casualty on either side was Black Kettle himself. His had been the difficult role of a Peace Chief. Probably the most prominent Cheyenne leader of the 1860s, he had done his utmost to protect his people, while somehow maintaining accord with the Whites. Four years earlier, his camp at Sand Creek in Colorado had been ruthlessly attacked by Colonel J.M. Chivington's Colorado Volunteers with about 150 Cheyenne and Arapaho men, women and children wantonly slaughtered.

In this attack, as the old Chief and his wife attempted to escape the onrush of Custer's troops, they were shot down while trying to cross the river and their bodies lay in the icy shallows of the Washita.

William L. English
Born 3 October 1840. Illinois.
1st Lieutenant, 7th Infantry.

Civil War Veteran, Volunteers, 1862 – 1865: Attained the rank of 1st Lieutenant, 101st Illinois Infantry. He served in Georgia and Tennessee during the war and was in action in a number of battles including Resaca, New Hope Church, Kennesaw Mountain, Peach Tree Creek, and the siege of Atlanta. Toward the war's end he participated in Sherman's Carolina Campaign. Honorably mustered out on 7 June, 1865.

Regular Army: *Commissioned 2nd Lieutenant, 7th Infantry, on 18 June, 1867. Promoted to 1st Lieutenant on 24 October, 1874. He served with Colonel Gibbon's Montana Column in the Sioux War of 1876.*

On 9 August, 1877, in Colonel John Gibbon's brutal fight with the Nez Perce at the battle of the Big Hole Basin, Montana, 1st Lieutenant English was mortally wounded. Transported from the field of battle by his comrades, he succumbed to his wounds on 20 August, 1877.

William J. Fetterman

Born c. 1833. Connecticut.
Captain, 27th Infantry.

Civil War Veteran, Regular Army: Commissioned 1st Lieutenant, 18th Infantry, on 14 May, 1861. Promoted to Captain on 25 October, 1861. During Sherman's Georgia Campaign, he fought in the battles of Resaca, Kennesaw Mountain, Peach Tree Creek, the siege of Atlanta, and Jonesboro.

Brevetted Major for gallant and meritorious conduct at Murfreesboro, Tennessee, on 31 December, 1862 and Lieutenant Colonel, on 1 September, 1864, for gallant and meritorious service in the Atlanta Campaign and at Jonesboro, Georgia.

Post-War Regular Army: *Transferred to the newly formed 27th Infantry on 21 September, 1866.*

In November 1866, Captain Fetterman was assigned to Fort Phil Kearny, Wyoming. This was one of the forts protecting the Bozeman Trail in Wyoming and Montana. The Sioux and Northern Cheyenne, through whose country the road passed, vigorously objected to the presence of the army posts in their midst. Colonel Carrington, Phil Kearny's commander, had assumed an essentially defensive role in dealing with the hostile Sioux led by the Oglala Chief Red Cloud.

Soon after his arrival, Captain Fetterman boldly

asserted that an aggressive approach was much more appropriate. Indeed, he claimed that given only eighty men, he could "ride through the Sioux Nation.[6]" Several of the other officers at the post, including Captain Fred Brown and 2nd Lieutenant G.W. Grummond, supported Fetterman's view.

After participating in an inconclusive fight with the hostiles on 6 December, Captain Fetterman, at his own request, was placed in command of troops assigned to relieve a wood cutting train under attack by the Sioux, a short distance from the fort, on the cold, gray morning of 21 December 1866. The command consisted of 81 men—3 officers, 76 enlisted men and two civilians.

Shortly after the troops exited the post, the Indians broke off the attack on the wood train and fell back beyond a point called Lodge Trail Ridge. The wood cutters then proceeded on their way unmolested. Though ordered by Colonel Carrington to return to the fort once the wood train was safe, Captain Fetterman instead pursued a few warriors he could see in the near distance. Just beyond Lodge Trail Ridge, the soldiers were attacked by overwhelming numbers of Sioux, Cheyenne and Arapaho warriors, led by High Backbone, Red Leaf, and Little Wolf. Among the decoy

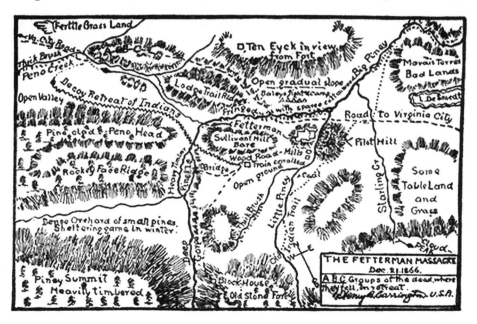

party was the young Oglala leader Crazy Horse.

Second Lieutenant Grummond and a few others were killed in the open, but Fetterman, Captain Brown and most of the men gained a reprieve by getting among some sandstone rocks. The now-dismounted cavalrymen probably caused a number of casualties among the Indians with their seven-shot Spencer carbines, before being overwhelmed by sheer numbers. Wheatley and Fisher, the two civilians, were each armed with new 16-shot Henry rifles. They appeared to have inflicted a heavy toll on their assailants before they died, for when their bodies were recovered, Colonel Carrington counted 65 splotches of blood in the snow around them.

As it was the custom of the Sioux and other Plains Indians to retrieve their dead after a battle, their real loss cannot be known.

As the Sioux and Cheyenne were about to overwhelm Fetterman's position, he and Captain Brown apparently shot each other in the head, rather than face capture and torture.

In 40 terrible minutes, the entire command was destroyed.

James H. French
Born 14 March, 1851. Pennsylvania.
Entered U.S.M.A. 1869.
2nd Lieutenant, 9th Cavalry.

Regular Army: *Graduated from the U.S. Military Academy and promoted to 2nd Lieutenant, 9th Cavalry, on 17 June, 1874. Served in Texas and Colorado until 31 August, 1876, when, because of ill health, he resigned his commission. Re-commissioned 2nd Lieutenant, 9th Cavalry, on 10 August, 1878.*

On 17 January, 1880, 2nd Lt. French was killed in a clash with Apaches under the redoubtable Mimbres leader, Victorio, in the San Mateo Mountains, New Mexico.

George W. Grummond
Michigan.
2nd Lieutenant, 18th Infantry.

Civil War Veteran, Volunteers, 1861 - 1865: Served with the 1st and 14th Michigan Infantry Regiments, attaining the rank of Lieutenant Colonel. Honorably mustered out on 18 July, 1865.

Regular Army: *Commissioned 2nd Lieutenant, 18th Infantry, on 7 May, 1866.*

Assigned to Fort Phil Kearny, Wyoming, 2nd Lieutenant Grummond narrowly escaped death in a spirited fight with the Sioux on 6 December, 1866. Finding himself surrounded by warriors, he had to hack his way through them with his saber. His respite was short-lived, however.

Fifteen days later, while commanding a company of the 2nd Cavalry, he was killed in the Fetterman Disaster.

Owen Hale
Born 29 July, 1843. New York.
Captain, 7th Cavalry.

Civil War Veteran, Volunteers, 1861 - 1865: Attained the rank of 1st Lieutenant, 7th New York Cavalry. Honorably mustered out on 29 November, 1865.

Brevetted Captain of Volunteers, on 13 March, 1865, for gallant and meritorious service during the War.

Regular Army: *Commissioned 1st Lieutenant, 7th Cavalry, on 28 July, 1866. Promoted to Captain on 1 March, 1869.*

On 27 November 1868, he participated in Custer's fight on the Washita River. Absent on detached duty in 1876, Captain Hale was not with his regiment at the Little Big Horn. The following year, near the end of the Nez Perce Campaign, he was killed on 30 September 1877, while leading his "K" Company and two others in a frontal assault on the enemy camp on Snake Creek, near the Bear Paw Mountains, Montana.

Minutes before the battle, when Colonel Miles had given the order to assault the well entrenched Indian positions, Captain Hale had exclaimed, "My God, have I got to go out and get killed in such cold weather?"[7]

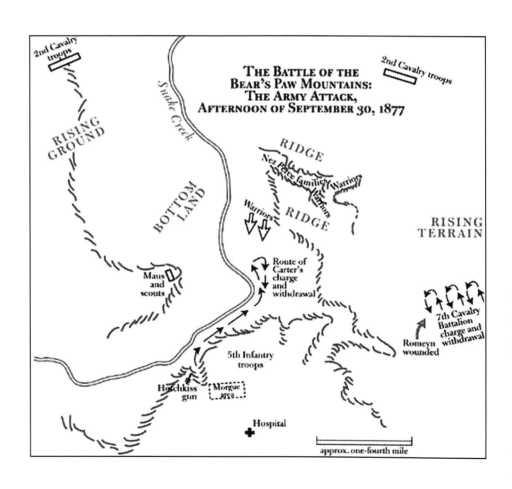

Louis M. Hamilton
Born 21 July, 1844. New York.
Captain, 7th Cavalry.

Civil War Veteran, Volunteers and Regular Army: Served as a Private in the 22nd New York State Militia and 14th U.S. Infantry. Commissioned 2nd Lieutenant, 3rd U.S. Infantry, on 27 September, 1862. Promoted to 1st Lieutenant on 6 May, 1864.

Brevetted 1st Lieutenant, on 3 May, 1863, for gallant and meritorious service at Chancellorsville, Virginia and Captain, on 2 July, 1863, for gallant and meritorious service at Gettysburg, Pennsylvania.

Post-War Regular Army: *Served as Regimental Quartermaster, 3rd Infantry, 1865-1866. Transferred to 7th Cavalry, and promoted to Captain, on 28 July, 1866.*

A grandson of statesman Alexander Hamilton, Captain Hamilton fought in the Hancock Campaign against the Southern Cheyenne and their Sioux allies in 1867 and in General Sully's Expedition against the Kiowa's and Comanche's the following year.

In response to Major General Phillip Sheridan's call for a winter offensive against the Southern Cheyenne and their allies, Custer's regiment was in the field in Western Oklahoma. On the snowy, bitter cold night of 26-27 November, 1868, Captain Hamilton was in command of Custer's supply train, when word was received from a scouting party that definite signs of an Indian camp had been located not many miles distant.

Not wishing to miss the coming fight, Captain Hamilton asked Lieutenant Colonel Custer's permission to take part in the assault, which was sure to follow, once the enemy was found. The commanding officer replied that he might go if he could find a replacement to command the train. First Lieutenant E.G. Mathey, who was scheduled to make the assault, was suffering from snow blindness, so he and Hamilton switched places.

A few hours before dawn, the entire regiment joined the scouts who had located a war trail leading toward the Washita. Shortly thereafter, an encampment of about 50 lodges was located on the banks of the river, and Custer ordered an attack at first light. In the opening moments of the battle, riding at Custer's side, Captain Hamilton was hit in the chest by one of the first shots, dying on the spot. Controversy exists as to the direction the shot came from, but the Surgeon's report supports it came from hostiles to his front.

Posthumously Brevetted Major, on 27 November, 1868, "for gallant and meritorious service in engagements with Indians, particularly in the battle with the Cheyenne on the Washita River, Indian Territory, 27 November, 1868, where he was killed while gallantly leading his command."[8]

Henry M. Harrington
Born 30 April, 1849. New York.
Entered U.S.M.A. 1868.
2nd Lieutenant, 7th Cavalry.

Regular Army: *Graduated from the U.S. Military Academy and promoted to 2nd Lieutenant, 7th Cavalry, on 14 June, 1872.*

Harrington was a member of the Yellowstone Expedition in 1873 and of the Black Hills Expedition the following year. While serving as the Executive Officer of "C" Company, under the command of Captain Thomas W. Custer, 2nd Lieutenant Harrington was listed as missing in action and presumed killed, at the Little Big Horn River, Montana, on 25 June, 1876.

In July 1877 an army medical officer found a nearly complete human skull on the Custer Battlefield which he donated to the Army Medical Museum. The specimen was later given to the Smithsonian Institute where it resided until 2004 when through the good intuition of researcher Walt Cross, and careful forensic analysis, the remains were confirmed to be those of Lieutenant Harrington.

George M. Harris
Born c. 1846. Pennsylvania.
Entered U.S.M.A. 1863.
1st Lieutenant, 4th Artillery.

Regular Army: Graduated from the U.S. Military Academy and promoted to 2nd Lieutenant, 10th Infantry, on 15 June, 1868. Unassigned 19 May, 1869. Assigned to the 4th Artillery on 14 July 1869. Promoted to 1st Lieutenant on 1 May, 1873.
      On 26 April, 1873, Lieutenant Harris was mortally wounded by Modoc's in the Thomas -Wright Massacre in the Lava Beds of Northern California. When informed by telegram of her son's fate, Harris' mother traveled from Pennsylvania by every available conveyance and reached his bedside on the evening of 11 May. The young officer died the following day.

Edmund C. Hentig
Born 24 August, 1842. Michigan.
Captain, 6th Cavalry.

Regular Army: Commissioned 2nd Lieutenant, 6th Cavalry, on 12 June, 1867. Promoted to 1st Lieutenant on 23 December, 1868 and to Captain, on 15 November, 1876.

In the summer of 1881, a White Mountain Apache

mystic named Noch-ay-del-Klinne, known to Whites for a decade as a harmless dreamer, started to draw considerable attention to himself. In the vicinity of Camp Apache, Arizona, he began holding spiritually oriented meetings attended by a growing number of Apaches.

Incorporating elements of Christianity, he preached that dead friends and family would soon be resurrected, the Whites driven out of the Indian lands, and that better days for all Apaches were just ahead. He taught the Apaches a special rhythmic dance and generally made them feel confident about themselves and the future. The Indian Scouts at Camp Apache were also deeply affected by Noch-ay-del-Klinne's message. They absented themselves from the post, without permission, to attend the meetings and became distant and surly with their officers when they returned.

Early in August, the agent at the San Carlos Agency, and General Carr at Camp Apache, invited the Prophet, as the Indian mystic had come to be called, to come in to talk. He refused them both. On 29 August, 1881, at the agent's urging, General Carr with 117 men, including Captain Hentig's "D" Company, 6th Cavalry, and 23 Apache Scouts, started from Camp Apache for the Prophet's camp on Cibicu Creek, about 35 miles distant. Carr was reluctant to use the Scouts but hoped that their presence would make the arrest of the Prophet easier.

The arrest was made without incident on the following day, though the situation was tense. That evening, however, when Carr had camped for the night, most of the Scouts and several of Noch-ay-del-Klinne's followers, who had trailed along behind the soldiers, suddenly opened fire on them. Captain Hentig was killed in the first volley, and six enlisted men were dead or mortally wounded within a few minutes. That night the Apaches broke off the action and disappeared in the darkness, having lost more than 20 men. Among the dead were six of the Scouts and Noch-ay-del-Klinne. Carr buried his dead and returned to Camp Apache the following day.

On 3 March, 1882, the army hanged three of the Scouts for their part in the "Cibicu Affair."

Benjamin H. Hodgson
Born 30 June, 1848.
Pennsylvania.
Entered U.S.M.A. 1865.
2nd Lieutenant, 7th Cavalry.

Regular Army: *Graduated from the U.S. Military Academy and promoted to 2nd Lieutenant, 7th Cavalry, on 15 June, 1870.*

He was a member of the Yellowstone Expedition in 1873 and the Black Hills Expedition the following year. While serving as the Adjutant to Major Marcus A. Reno, 2nd Lieutenant Hodgson was killed in the rout of Reno's Battalion by Sioux and Northern Cheyenne warriors at the Little Big Horn River, Montana, on 25 June 1876.

In the headlong race across the river, Hodgson's horse was killed and the Lieutenant wounded in both legs. Shouting, "For God's sake, don't leave me here!,"[9] he seized the stirrup of a passing trooper's horse and was dragged to the far bank where he was killed by a shot to the head.

A jovial and very likeable man, his loss was felt by the whole regiment.

Albion Howe
Born c. 1841. Florida.
1st Lieutenant, 4th Artillery.

Civil War Veteran, Volunteers, 1863 - 1865: Attained the rank of Major, 14th New York Artillery. Honorably mustered out on 26 August, 1865.

Regular Army: Commissioned 2nd Lieutenant, 4th Artillery, on 1

December, 1866. Promoted to 1st Lieutenant on 18 November, 1869.

Brevetted 1st Lieutenant and Captain respectively, on 2 March, 1867, for gallant and distinguished service at the battle of Cold Harbor and at Petersburg, Virginia.

The son of Civil War General A.P. Howe, 1st Lieutenant Howe was killed in the Thomas-Wright Massacre by Modoc Indians in the Lava Beds, Northern California, on 26 April, 1873.

John C. Jenness
Vermont.
1st Lieutenant, 27th Infantry.

Civil War Veteran, Volunteers, 1862 - 1865: Served with the 17th New Hampshire Infantry and 1st New Hampshire Artillery, attaining the rank of 1st Lieutenant. Honorably mustered out on 15 June, 1865.

Regular Army: *Commissioned 2nd Lieutenant, 27th Infantry, on 28 July, 1866. Promoted to 1st Lieutenant on 5 March, 1867.*

On 2 August, 1867, in the celebrated Wagon Box Fight near Fort Phil Kearny, Wyoming, 1st Lieutenant Jenness was shot through the head and instantly killed by fire from Oglala and Minneconjou warriors under Red Cloud and High Backbone.

This spirited battle was fought by approximately 32 soldiers and civilians in a good defensive position inside a corral made of wagon bodies against possibly a thousand Sioux. In addition to Lieutenant Jenness, the soldiers lost five privates killed and two wounded. Commanding Officer, Capt James Powell, 27th Infantry, estimated Red Cloud lost about 180 men, with roughly 60 being killed. The actual numbers are uncertain, and likely much less.[10]

Springfield "Trap Door" Rifle as issued to the 27th Infantry in time for the "Wagon Box Fight." Converted from the M1861 muzzle loading version into a breech loading, cartridge firing weapon, it's previous rate of fire was at least tripled, making it almost impossible for "hostiles" to come to close quarters against such firepower.

The soldiers' success was largely based on the fact that they were armed with the new quick-firing, cartridge-fed "trap door" Springfield-Allin Model 1866 .50-70 rifles—a far cry from the original slow, cumbersome, muzzle loading Civil War Springfield's with which Captain Fetterman's Infantry were armed in the disastrous fight the previous December.

Myles W. Keogh
Born 25 March, 1842. Ireland.
Captain, 7th Cavalry.

Foreign Service: *The son of an officer in the Royal Irish Lancers, he entered service in 1860 as a 2nd Lieutenant in the Battalion of St. Patrick of the Papal Army in Italy and later served as a Lieutenant in the Papal Guards of the Vatican. He was recognized and decorated with the Order of St. Gregory the Great for his distinguished service and bravery against the enemies of the Papacy.*

Civil War Veteran, Volunteers, 1862 - 1866: Immigrating to the United States in 1862, he was on 9 April of that year appointed a Captain of U.S. Volunteers. During the Civil War he served on the staffs of Union generals Patterson, Shields, Buford, and Stoneman, and was promoted to Major, aide-de-camp, Volunteers, on 7 April, 1864. He served in both the Eastern and Western Theatres and saw action in thirty general engagements including Port Republic, 2nd Bull Run, Chantilly, South Mountain, Antietam, Kelly's Ford, Brandy Station, Kennesaw Mountain, and Resaca.

Honorably mustered out of the Volunteers on 1 September, 1866. Brevetted Lieutenant Colonel of Volunteers, 13 March, 1865, for uniform gallantry and good conduct during the War.

Regular Army: *Commissioned 2nd Lieutenant, 4th Cavalry, on 4 May, 1866. Transferred to the 7th Cavalry, and promoted to Captain, on 28 July, 1866. Brevetted Major and Lieutenant Colonel respectively, on 2 March, 1867, for gallant and meritorious service in the battles of Gettysburg, Pennsylvania and Dallas, Georgia.*

A Captain with the 7th since its inception, Myles Keogh is generally credited with having suggested that the lively Irish tavern song "Garryowen" be adopted as the new regiment's official marching anthem.

In 1867, during General Hancock's Campaign against the Southern Cheyenne and their Sioux allies, Captain Keogh served as Post Commander at Fort Wallace, Kansas. He was a member of Sully's Expedition against the Kiowa's and Comanche's in 1868 but was not with his regiment at the Washita. In 1873 and 1874, he served as a member of the military escort for the Northern Boundary Survey Commission.

The commander of "I" Company, the Custer Battalion, Captain Keogh was killed in action with Sioux and Northern Cheyenne warriors at the Little Big Horn River,

"Comanche," easily the best known survivor of Little Big Horn (other horses were recovered). Never ridden again, and provided a bucket of beer every Sunday for the rest of his life, he lived in honored retirement, passing on November 7, 1891, around 29 years old.

Montana, 25 June, 1876. Keogh's horse, "Comanche," was found wounded on the Custer Battlefield, restored to health, and never ridden again. For many years he was led in military parades, with boots turned backward in the stirrups, in memory of the Captain and those who fell with him.

Lyman S. Kidder

Born 31 August, 1842. Vermont.
2nd Lieutenant, 2nd Cavalry.

Civil War Veteran, Volunteers, 1861 - 1866: Served with the 5th Iowa and 1st Minnesota Cavalry Regiments and in Hatch's Battalion of Minnesota Cavalry, attaining the ranks of 1st Sergeant and 1st Lieutenant. He was in several actions against the Eastern Sioux in Minnesota in 1863, during the Little Crow Uprising. Honorably mustered out of the Volunteers on 1 May, 1866.

Regular Army: *Commissioned 2nd Lieutenant, 2nd Cavalry, on 22 January, 1867.*

THE FATE OF LIEUT. KIDDER AND HIS ENTIRE COMMAND—DISCOVERY OF THEIR BODIES.

In late June 1867, 2nd Lieutenant Kidder, with an escort of ten troopers and an Indian Scout, left Fort Sedgwick, Colorado with orders for Lieutenant Colonel G.A. Custer, who was encamped on the Republican River in Kansas.

On about 2 July, near Beaver Creek in Northwest Kansas, the escort was set upon by a large war party of Sioux warriors and Cheyenne Dog Soldiers. There were no survivors. Custer discovered the savagely mutilated bodies of Kidder and his men days later and buried them with honors.

William H. Lewis
Born c. 1829. Alabama.
Entered U.S.M.A. 1845. Lieutenant Colonel, 19th Infantry.

Regular Army: *Graduated from the U.S. Military Academy as a Brevet 2nd Lieutenant, 4th Infantry, on 1 July 1849. Promoted to 2nd Lieutenant, 1st Infantry, on 31 August 1849. Transferred to the 5th Infantry in 1850. Promoted to 1st Lieutenant on 3 March, 1855 and served as Regimental Adjutant, 1856-1857.*

His pre-Civil War experiences included fighting the Seminoles in 1856-1857, serving on Colonel A.S. Johnston's Utah Expedition against the Mormons, 1857-1859 and in campaigns against the Navajos in 1860-1861.

Civil War Veteran, Regular Army: Promoted to Captain on 7 May 1861 and to Major, 18th Infantry, on 14 July 1864.

Brevetted Major, on 28 March, 1862, for gallant and meritorious service at Apache Canyon, New Mexico and Lieutenant Colonel, on 15 April, 1862, for gallant and meritorious service

.45-70 Rounds for the "Trapdoor" Springfield Rifle of the US. Infantry.

at Peralta, New Mexico.

Post-War Regular Army: *Transferred to the 36th Infantry on 21 September, 1866. Transferred to the 7th Infantry on 15 March, 1869. Promoted to Lieutenant Colonel, 19th Infantry, on 10 December, 1873.*

Between 1871 and 1874, he served as Special Inspector and Acting Assistant Inspector General for the Department of Dakota and as Military Commander of Baton Rouge, Louisiana.

On 27 September, 1878, in the opening phase of the army's pursuit of Northern Cheyenne fleeing their reservation in Oklahoma, troops commanded by Lieutenant Colonel Lewis clashed with the Indians at the Punished Woman's Fork of the Smoky Hill River in central Kansas. Mortally wounded in this action, Lewis died the following day while being conveyed in an ambulance to Fort Wallace, Kansas.

William Logan
Born 9 December, 1832. Ireland. Captain, 7th Infantry.

Civil War Veteran, Regular Army: Enlisted as a Private, 7th Infantry, on 27 December, 1850 and promoted to Sergeant on the same date. Participated in the sanguinary engagement at Fredericksburg, Virginia, 13 December, 1862. Served as a Hospital Steward, 1863 - 1864. Commissioned a 2nd Lieutenant and promoted to 1st Lieutenant, on 18 May, 1864. Served as Regimental Quartermaster, 1864-1869. Promoted to Captain on 24 October, 1874.

Captain Logan commanded "A" Company, 7th Infantry, in Colonel Gibbon's Montana Column during the Sioux War of 1876. The following year, on 9 August, he was shot through the head while in action with Nez Perce Indians at the Big Hole Basin, Montana.

George E. Lord
Born 17 February, 1846.
Massachusetts.
Assistant Surgeon, U.S. Army.

Regular Army: *He entered service as a civilian contract surgeon practicing on several frontier posts between 1871 and 1875. In 1874, he was Acting Assistant Surgeon with the 6th Infantry while it served as escort for the Northern Boundary Survey Commission.*

Dr. Lord was commissioned 1st Lieutenant, Assistant Surgeon, on 26 June, 1875 and assigned to the 7th Cavalry. While attached to the Custer Battalion, he was killed at the Little Big Horn River, Montana, on 25 June, 1876.

John Madagan
Born c. 1840. Ireland.
1st Lieutenant, 1st Cavalry.

Civil War Veteran, Volunteers, 1861 - 1865: Served with the 88th New York Infantry and 2nd New Jersey Cavalry, attaining the rank of 1st Lieutenant. Honorably mustered out on 1 November, 1865.

Regular Army: *Commissioned 2nd Lieutenant, 1st Cavalry, on 23 February, 1866. Promoted to 1st Lieutenant on 25 April, 1867.*

On 27 September, 1867, 1st Lieutenant Madagan was killed in action with Pitt River and Northern Paiute Indians in a hard fight at the Infernal Caverns in Northern California. Afterwards, Colonel George Crook, the expedition commander, said of Madagan, "A braver officer never lived."[11]

Posthumously Brevetted Captain, on 27 September, 1867, for conspicuous gallantry in his last action.

Thomas J.C. Maddox
Born 12 December, 1852. Maryland.
Assistant Surgeon, U.S. Army.

Regular Army: *Commissioned Assistant Surgeon, U.S. Army, on 22 October, 1881.*

While attached to an escort of the 8th Cavalry on 19 December 1885, Surgeon Maddox was ambushed with four troopers by Chiracahua Apaches led by Ulzana, near White House (or Little Dry Creek), New Mexico. Shot in the stomach, Maddox dismounted and calmly said to a nearby trooper, "Babcock, save yourself. I shall be dead in a minute."[12]

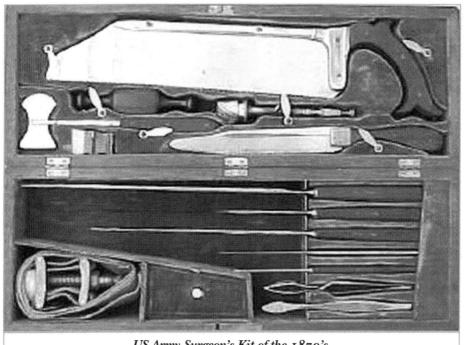

US Army Surgeon's Kit of the 1870's.

James D. Mann
Born 15 May, 1854. Indiana.
Entered U.S.M.A. 1873.
1st Lieutenant, 7th Cavalry.

__Regular Army:__ Graduated from the U.S. Military Academy and commissioned 2nd Lieutenant, 7th Cavalry, on 15 June, 1877. Promoted to 1st Lieutenant on 22 July, 1890.

On 30 December, 1890, only one day after his company commander, Captain Wallace, was killed at Wounded Knee, 1st Lieutenant Mann was mortally wounded in a sharp clash with the Sioux near White Clay Creek, South Dakota.

Succumbing on 15 January, 1891, Lieutenant Mann was the last regular officer to be killed in the long struggle with the Sioux, and the last, but one, to perish in the Indian Wars.

Donald McIntosh
Born 4 September, 1838. Canada.
1st Lieutenant, 7th Cavalry.

His mother, Charlotte Robinson, was a direct descendent of the Seneca Iroquois Chief Red Jacket. His father, James McIntosh, an employee of the Hudson's Bay Company, was killed by Indians when Donald was only 14.

Between 1846 and 1860 he lived and worked on the various posts of the famous trading company. During the Civil War he served as chief civilian clerk for Union Army Colonel David H. Rucker.

Regular Army: Commissioned 2nd Lieutenant, 7th Cavalry, on 17 August, 1867. Promoted to 1st Lieutenant on 22 March, 1870.

1st Lieutenant McIntosh was commanding "G" Company when he was cut off from his men and killed by Sioux warriors in the rout of Major Reno's Battalion at the Little Big Horn on 25 June, 1876. When recovered on 27 June, his body was found to be terribly mutilated. An educated, well-liked and respected man, he was at 37 the oldest and probably the first officer to fall at the Little Big Horn.

John A. McKinney
Born c. 1846. Tennessee.
Entered U.S.M.A. 1867. 1st Lieutenant, 4th Cavalry.

Regular Army: Graduated from the U.S. Military Academy and commissioned 2nd Lieutenant, 4th Cavalry, on 12 June, 1871. Promoted to 1st Lieutenant on 17 May, 1876.

On 29 September, 1872, while serving with the 4th in Texas, he was involved in a sharp, and for the Comanche's, costly fight near the mouth of McClellan Creek on the North Fork of the Red River.

On 25 November, 1876, Lt. McKinney participated in the U.S. Army's Powder River Expedition against the Sioux and their allies. While leading his Company through a deep ravine during Colonel Ranald S. MacKenzie's cavalry assault on Dull Knife and Little Wolf's camp of Northern Cheyenne on the North Fork of Wyoming's Powder River, McKinney was ambushed, struck by six bullets and killed.

It was reported that Colonel MacKenzie, the 4th's commander, was visibly moved when informed of this courageous officer's death.

James F. Millar
New York.
Captain, 14th Infantry.

Civil War Veteran, Regular Army: Served very briefly as a Private in the 2nd Ohio Infantry. Commissioned 1st Lieutenant, 14th Infantry, on 14 May, 1861. Promoted to Captain on 17 September, 1862.

Brevetted Major, on 1 August, 1864, for gallant and meritorious service at the battle of the Wilderness, Virginia.

Transferred to the Southwest after the war, Captain Millar and four of his men were ambushed and killed by Apaches near Cottonwood Springs, Arizona, on 22 March, 1866. When attacked, the escort was en route from Fort Yuma to Fort Grant, Arizona. Assistant Surgeon Benjamin Tappan also died as a result of this incident.

Seward Mott
Born 21 August, 1861. New York.
Entered U.S.M.A 1881.
2nd Lieutenant, 10th Cavalry.

Regular Army: *Graduated from the U.S. Military Academy and commissioned 2nd Lieutenant, 6th Cavalry, on 1 July, 1886. Transferred to the 10th Cavalry on 6 July, 1886.*

Assigned to the San Carlos Indian Reservation,

Nahdeizaz immediately prior to his execution. Note the absence of a "trap door scaffold" in favor of a heavy counterweight drawing the condemned up.

Arizona, part of the Lieutenant's task was to instruct Apaches in farming and irrigation methods.

On 10 March, 1887, he fell into a dispute with an Apache named Nahdeizaz, who mortally wounded the officer, who died the following day. Nahdeizaz was hanged for the murder by order of an army court, on 27 December, 1889.

James E. Porter
Born 2 February, 1847. Maine.
Entered U.S.M.A. 1864.
1st Lieutenant, 7th Cavalry.

Regular Army: *Graduated from the U.S. Military Academy and commissioned 2nd Lieutenant, 7th Cavalry, on 15 June, 1869. Promoted to 1st Lieutenant on 1 March, 1872.*

During 1873 and 1874, he served as an escort officer for the Northern Boundary Survey. First Lieutenant Porter was the Executive Officer of Captain Keogh's "I" Company, the Custer Battalion, when he was killed in action with Sioux and Northern Cheyenne warriors at the Little Big Horn River, Montana, on 25 June, 1876.

Though his body was never identified, his bloody jacket, punctured by several bullet holes, was found two days after the battle in the abandoned Indian camp.

The only surviving Guidon found on the Custer Battlefield shortly after the battle.

Sevier M. Rains

Born c. 1851. Michigan.
Entered U.S.M.A. 1872.
2nd Lieutenant, 1st Cavalry.

Regular Army: *Graduated from the U.S. Military Academy and commissioned 2nd Lieutenant, 1st Cavalry, on 15 June, 1876.*

Near Craig's Mountain, Idaho, on 3 July, 1877, 2nd Lieutenant Rains, with a detachment of 11 men, was searching for a wounded scout when attacked by Nez Perce under Five Wounds. The whole detachment was quickly annihilated by typically deadly rifle fire of these warriors.

William V. W. Reily

Born 12 December, 1853.
Washington, D.C.
2nd Lieutenant, 7th Cavalry.

Regular Army: *Commissioned 2nd Lieutenant, 10th Cavalry, on 15 October, 1875. Transferred to the 7th Cavalry on 26 January, 1876.*

While acting as Executive Officer of "F" Company, the Custer Battalion, he was killed in action with Sioux and Northern Cheyenne warriors at the Little Big Horn River, Montana, on 25 June, 1876.

Remington single shot breech loading rifle. While never adopted by the US Army, it was a popular design that saw wide usage by Indians and settlers alike, as well as sold in various calibers to powers from Russia to Egypt.

Levi H. Robinson
Vermont.
1st Lieutenant, 14th Infantry.

Civil War Veteran, Volunteers and Regular Army, 1862 - 1866: Served most of the conflict as a Sergeant of the 10th Vermont Infantry but entered the 119th U.S. Colored Infantry with the rank of 2nd Lieutenant, from 18 February, 1865, until honorably mustered out on 27 April, 1866.

Post-War Regular Army: *Commissioned 2nd Lieutenant, 14th Infantry, on 19 April, 1866. Promoted to 1st Lieutenant on 11 August, 1866.*

On 9 February, 1874, while providing an escort for a lumber train at Cottonwood Creek, near Laramie Peak, Wyoming, 1st Lieutenant Robinson and the Corporal of his detachment were set upon and killed by Sioux Indians.

Camp Robinson, Nebraska, which gained prominence later in the Plains War, was named in honor of the slain officer only a few weeks after his death.

William Russell, Jr.
New York.
2nd Lieutenant, 4th Cavalry.

Civil War Veteran, Volunteers, 1861 - 1866: Served as 1st Lt. and Regimental Quartermaster with the 18th New York Infantry, 1861-1863 and was Major and Assistant Adjutant General of Volunteers from 1863, until honorably mustered out on 10 February, 1866. Brevetted Lieutenant

Colonel of Volunteers, on 13 March, 1865, for meritorious service during the War.

Regular Army: *Commissioned 2nd Lieutenant, 4th Cavalry, on 25 October, 1867.*

Brevetted 1st Lieutenant, Captain and Major respectively, on 25 October, 1867, for gallant and meritorious service in the battles of Antietam, Maryland, Gettysburg, Pennsylvania and Petersburg, Virginia.

On 14 May, 1870, 2nd Lieutenant Russell was commanding a detachment of "M" Company, 4th Cavalry, when he was mortally wounded in action with unidentified Indians at Mount Adams, Texas. He died the following day.

William L. Sherwood
New York.
1st Lieutenant, 21st Infantry.

Regular Army: *Commissioned 2nd Lieutenant, 21st Infantry, on 3 September, 1867. Promoted to 1st Lieutenant on 22 July, 1872.*

A casualty of the costly Modoc War, 1st Lieutenant Sherwood was mortally wounded by Modoc's, while he and a second officer were in the act of receiving a flag of truce from them, in the Lava Beds, Northern California, on 11 April, 1873.

Only minutes later, the party of Peace Commissioners was also treacherously attacked and General Canby and Reverend Eleasar Thomas brutally murdered.

First Lieutenant Sherwood succumbed to his wounds on 14 April, 1873.

Modoc's defending the Lava Beds and depicted with reasonable accuracy in the popular press.

Algernon E. Smith

Born 17 September, 1842.
New York.
1st Lieutenant, 7th Cavalry.

Civil War Veteran, Volunteers, 1862 - 1865: Served with the 117th New York Infantry, attaining the rank of Captain, and as aide-de-camp to General Alfred Terry. He saw combat in the Carolinas and Virginia, participating in actions at Fort Wagner, Cold Harbor, Petersburg, and Fort Fisher, where he was severely wounded while leading an assault. As a result, one arm remained permanently crippled. Honorably mustered out of the Volunteers on 15 May, 1865.

Brevetted Major of Volunteers, on 13 March, 1865, for gallant and meritorious service at the storming of Fort Fisher, North Carolina.

Regular Army: *Commissioned 2nd Lieutenant, 7th Cavalry, on 9 August 1867. Promoted to 1st Lieutenant on 5 December, 1868. Served as Regimental Quartermaster in 1869.*

Brevetted 1st Lieutenant and Captain respectively, on 9 August, 1867, for gallant and meritorious service at Drury's Farm, Virginia and for the capture of Fort Fisher, North Carolina.

Lieutenant Smith was with his regiment in Custer's fight on the Washita River in 1868 and participated in the Yellowstone Expedition of 1873. In 1874 he served as Quartermaster on the Black Hills Expedition.

On 25 June, 1876, while acting as the commander of "E" Company, the Custer Battalion, 1st Lieutenant Smith was killed in action with Sioux and Northern Cheyenne warriors at the Little Big Horn River, Montana.

Lakota Chief Kicking Bear's Depiction (1898) of the end of Custer's Battalion.

George W. Smith
Born 11 March, 1837.
Virginia.
2nd Lieutenant, 9th Cavalry.

Civil War Veteran, Regular Army: Commissioned Captain, 18th Infantry, on 5 August, 1861. Resigned 15 May, 1866.

Brevetted Major, on 20 September, 1863, for gallant and meritorious service at Chickamauga, Georgia and Lieutenant Colonel, on 1 September, 1864, for gallant and meritorious service during the Atlanta Campaign and at Jonesboro, Georgia.

Post-War Regular Army: *Commissioned 2nd Lieutenant, 9th Cavalry, on 6 August, 1873.*

On 19 August, 1881, 2nd Lieutenant Smith and four enlisted men were killed by Mimbres Apaches led by Nana in a fight near McEver's Ranch, New Mexico.

Charles B. Stambaugh
Ohio.
1st Lieutenant, 2nd Cavalry.

Civil War Veteran, Volunteers, 1864 - 1866: Served in the enlisted ranks of the 11th Ohio Cavalry. Honorably mustered out of the Volunteers on 2 May, 1866.

Regular Army: *Commissioned 2nd Lieutenant, 2nd Cavalry, on 7 March, 1867. Promoted to 1st Lieutenant on 5 July, 1868.*

On 4 May, 1870, 1st Lieutenant Stambaugh was killed in a hard fight with Northern Arapaho's at Miner's Delight, near Twin Creek, Wyoming.

Sigismund Sternberg
Born c.1837. Prussia.
2nd Lieutenant, 27th Infantry.

Civil War Veteran, Volunteers and Regular Army, 1862 - 1866: Served with the 175th and 7th New York Infantry Regiments, attaining the rank of Captain. Honorably mustered out of the Volunteers on 4 August, 1865. He then served as an officer of the Regular Army in the 82nd U.S. Colored Infantry from 10 September, 1865 until 10 September, 1866 when, having attained the rank of Captain, he was honorably mustered out for the second time.

Post-War Regular Army:
Re-entered the Army as a 2nd Lieutenant, 27th Infantry, on 7 March, 1867.

On 1 August, 1867, 2nd Lieutenant Sternberg was commanding a detachment of 19 men

US Infantry Insignia, 1872-1875

charged with protecting civilian hay cutters near Fort C.F. Smith, Montana, when attacked by at least 500 Sioux and Northern Cheyenne. In the opening moments of this action, remembered as the Hayfield Fight, Lieutenant Sternberg was killed by a shot through the head while urging his men to stand up and fight like soldiers.

Sternberg's soldiers and the civilian workers, together numbering about 25 men, took cover inside a fortified corral prepared for the purpose and held off the enemy for about eight hours, until relieved by troops from the fort.

The defenders, using new breech-loading Springfield and Henry rifles, were able to inflict numerous casualties on the attacking force, with the loss of only one other soldier and one civilian killed and several men wounded.

The following day and 95 miles distant, another detachment of the 27th Infantry fought a similar engagement with the Sioux, with comparable results, near Fort Phil Kearny, Wyoming. (See John C. Jenness, pg. 52).

Reid T. Stewart
Born c. 1850. Pennsylvania.
Entered U.S.M.A. 1867.
2nd Lieutenant, 5th Cavalry.

Regular Army: *Graduated from the U.S. Military Academy and promoted to 2nd Lieutenant, 5th Cavalry, on 12 June, 1871.*

On 27 August, 1872, in an effort to reach a court-martial in Tucson, Arizona, where he was to appear as a witness, 2nd Lieutenant Stewart unwisely chose to ride in a mule-driven buckboard from Camp Crittenden through Apache-dominated Davidson's Canyon accompanied by only one Corporal.

Well into the canyon, the men were ambushed and Stewart instantly killed by gunfire. The Corporal, an experienced soldier named Black, who had cautioned against leaving the cavalry escort behind, was captured and tortured to death.

James G. Sturgis
Born 24 January, 1854.
New Mexico Territory.
Entered U.S.M.A. 1871.
2nd Lieutenant, 7th Cavalry.

Regular Army: Graduated from the U.S. Military Academy and promoted to 2nd Lieutenant, 7th Cavalry, on 16 June, 1875.

The son of Samuel Sturgis, the 7th's full Colonel, 2nd Lieutenant Sturgis was serving with "E" Company, the Custer Battalion, when he was listed as missing in action and presumed killed, at the Little Big Horn River, Montana, on 25 June, 1876.

Benjamin Tappan
Born 18 November, 1840. Ohio.
Assistant Surgeon, U.S. Army.

Civil War Veteran, Volunteers, 1861 – 1862: Served briefly as an acting hospital steward with the 8th Ohio Infantry. Honorably mustered out on 24 March, 1862 to attend medical school.

Regular Army: *After graduating from New York's Bellevue Hospital Medical College, he entered the army as an Assistant Surgeon on 3 December, 1864.*

The nephew of Edwin Stanton, Lincoln's Secretary of War, Surgeon Tappan was traveling with a small military escort when it was attacked by Tonto or Pinal Apaches near Cottonwood Springs, Arizona, on 22 March, 1866. Captain J.F. Millar, 14th Infantry, and four men were killed, and Tappan was badly wounded. He was left in the care of a teamster while other survivors went for help. These men lost their way, and the relief party did not reach the site until 26 March.

Captain Millar and his men were buried, but the wounded surgeon was never found. The fate of the teamster is unclear as well.

Edward R. Theller

Born c. 1831. Vermont.
1st Lieutenant, 21st Infantry.

Civil War Veteran, Volunteers, 1861 – 1866: Elected Captain, 2nd California Infantry, on 25 October, 1861 and retained this rank throughout the War. Honorably mustered out on 10 May, 1866.

Brevetted Major of Volunteers, on 13 March, 1865, for faithful and meritorious service during the War.

Regular Army: Commissioned 2nd Lieutenant, 9th Infantry, on 7 March, 1867. Transferred to the 21st Infantry on 30 August, 1869. Promoted to 1st Lieutenant on 31 August, 1871. He saw active service in the Modoc Campaign in 1873.

Described by General Oliver O. Howard as "a generous, brave man with a warm heart,"[13] 1st Lieutenant Theller was killed with 18 of his men, when his skirmish line was overwhelmed by the deadly accurate rifle fire of Nez Perce warriors, at White Bird Canyon, Idaho, on 17 June 1877.

This battle, which was a clear victory for the Indians, was the first military action of the arduous Nez Perce War.

Evan Thomas
Born December, 1843.
Washington, D.C.
Captain, 4th Artillery.

Civil War Veteran, Regular Army: Commissioned 2nd Lieutenant, 4th Artillery, on 9 April, 1861. Promoted to 1st Lieutenant on 14 May, 1861 and to Captain, on 31 August, 1864.

Brevetted Captain, on 13 December, 1862, for gallant and meritorious service at Fredericksburg, Virginia, and then to Major, on 3 July, 1863, for the same service at Gettysburg, Pennsylvania.

Five months into the expensive and frustrating Modoc War, the U.S. Army had accomplished nothing in the way of persuading the Indian leader, Keintpoos, better known to the Whites as "Captain Jack," to negotiate, surrender or be pried out of his excellent defensive position in the rugged Lava Beds of Northern California.

The Indian force, composed of approximately 60 warriors and their families, had managed to repulse several assaults by a numerically stronger army force, in addition to murdering Peace Commissioners General E.R.S. Canby and Reverend Eleasar Thomas, a Methodist minister.

On 26 April, 1873, Captain Evan Thomas was ordered to lead a 64 man patrol into the Lava Beds to investigate any Modoc activity. After advancing four miles into the Beds and seeing no sign of the enemy, Thomas unaccountably ordered his men to sit down in the open to have dinner.

Suddenly, a contingent of warriors led by Scarface Charley opened fire from concealed positions in the nearby rocks. After about two hours, a third of the men, including Thomas, his co-commander, Lieutenant Wright, and the three other officers present were either dead or dying. A number of the men not seriously wounded fled the four miles to safety. The surviving wounded were recovered two days later. This debâcle, in which not one Modoc died, is remembered as the Thomas-Wright Massacre.

Thomas T. Thornburgh
Born c. 1843. Tennessee. Entered U.S.M.A. 1863. Major, 4th Infantry.

Civil War Veteran, Volunteers, 1862 – 1863: Served with the Federal 6th Tennessee Infantry, attaining the rank of Sergeant Major. He saw action in the fierce battle of Stone's River, Tennessee, 31 December, 1862 to 2 January, 1863. Released from the Volunteers to enter the U.S. Military Academy in July, 1863.

Regular Army: *Graduated from the Military Academy and promoted to 2nd Lieutenant, 2nd Artillery, on 17 June, 1867 and to 1st Lieutenant, on 21 April, 1870. Promoted to Major, Paymaster, on 26 April, 1875. Transferred as Major to the 4th Infantry on 23 May, 1878.*

From 1871 to 1873, he was Professor of Military Science at East Tennessee State University. In 1878 he saw service against the Northern Cheyenne during the Dull Knife Episode.

In the fall of 1879, Major Thornburgh was Post Commander at Fort Fred Steele, Wyoming. On 29 September, while leading troops to investigate reports of misconduct by the Ute's at the White River Indian Agency, his immediate command of about 120 men encountered a force of somewhere between 100 and 300 Ute's blocking their advance near Milk Creek, Colorado, on the northern edge of the Ute Agency.

Thornburgh tried to parley with the Indians, but shots were fired, and the Major quickly deployed his troops for battle. The commander then attempted to ride alone back to his supply train, which was located some distance to the rear, to organize it for defense, but he was shot and killed by a Ute marksman within 500 yards of the wagons.

The cavalrymen then fell back to the corralled wagons, where they withstood numerous enemy assaults for a week, until the arrival of fresh troops under Colonel Wesley Merritt, 5th Cavalry, raised the siege and ended the battle. The soldiers suffered nine killed in addition to Major Thornburgh, while the Ute's suffered the loss of 37 warriors.

Shortly afterwards, General William T. Sherman, Commander of the Army, wrote of Thornburgh, "He was young, ardent, ambitious, of good judgment, and no man could have done better in life, nor met death with more heroism."[14]

Contemporary depiction of the action which began with Thornburgh's death.

Frederick R. Vincent
Prince Edward Island, Canada.
1st Lieutenant, 9th Cavalry.

Civil War Veteran, Volunteers, 1862 – 1865: Served in the 11th and 2nd Missouri State Militia Cavalry regiments, attaining the rank of Captain. Honorably mustered out on 29 March, 1865.

Regular Army: *Commissioned 2nd Lieutenant, 9th Cavalry, on 18 June, 1867. Promoted to 1st Lieutenant on 16 July, 1869.*

On the afternoon of 20 April, 1872, Kiowa raiders led by Big Bow and White Horse slaughtered 11 members of a government contractor's wagon train at Howard Wells, Texas. The Indians were immediately pursued by elements of two companies of the 9th Cavalry under Captain Michael Cooney. He caught up with the hostiles only eight miles from the site of the massacre.

The Kiowa's, in an excellent defensive position behind some rocks, immediately opened a concentrated fire on the troopers, killing several horses and wounding 1st Lieutenant Vincent, "H" Company's commander, through both legs.

After exchanging some ineffective fire with the Indians, Captain Cooney decided that with night fast approaching and his ammunition running low, it would be prudent to break off action and return to Howard Wells.

Lieutenant Vincent died that evening from loss of blood.

Spencer .50 caliber M1865 repeating carbine, a proven weapon widely used by the US Cavalry during and after the Civil War. A tubular magazine holding seven cartridges was loaded through the butt end of the weapon, and worked by depressing the lever after each shot. For all its advantages, the Army's preference for single shot weapons saw it replaced by the Springfield "Trap Door" Carbine in 1874.

George D. Wallace
Born 29 June, 1849.
South Carolina.
Entered U.S.M.A. 1868.
Captain, 7th Cavalry.

Regular Army: *Graduated from the U.S. Military Academy and promoted to 2nd Lieutenant, 7th Cavalry, on 14 June, 1872. Promoted to 1st Lieutenant on 25 June, 1876. Served as Regimental Adjutant, 1876 – 1877. Promoted to Captain on 23 September, 1885.*

Wallace participated in the Yellowstone Expedition of 1873 and commanded the Indian Scouts during the Black Hills Expedition of 1874. He served in Reno's Battalion at the Little Big Horn in 1876 and in the Nez Perce Campaign the following year.

In December 1890, at the height of the native spiritual movement called the Ghost Dance Religion, one of its adherents, a Minneconjou Sioux Chief named Big Foot, was traveling with 350 of his people, including about 40 Hunkpappa's, from his reservation on the Cheyenne River to join fellow believers at the Pine Ridge Agency, South Dakota. On the evening of the 28th they were intercepted by troops of the 7th Cavalry and camped for the night at Wounded Knee Creek, about 20 miles east of Pine Ridge.

The following morning, Colonel J.W. Forsyth surrounded the Sioux camp with 500 troopers. He then began the task of searching for hidden firearms among the Indians after his demand that all weapons be surrendered had produced dismal results. Forsyth was under orders from one of his superiors, Brigadier General John R. Brooke, to disarm the Minneconjou's and arrest Big Foot, who was considered a key figure in the unrest caused by the Ghost Dance movement. Finally, Big Foot's band was to be transported to Nebraska for resettlement.

The background to all this began more than a year earlier with the rise of a messianic figure among the Paiutes in Nevada. A young man named Wovoka began to teach a peaceful religion, which combined elements of native beliefs and Christianity, similar to the teaching of the Apache mystic, Noch-ay-del-Klinne, almost a decade earlier (see Edmond C. Hentig, p.49). The central theme of Wovoka's teaching was that the Indians would soon be restored to their old way of life, except there would be no more death. The buffalo herds would return, friends and relatives who had died would be brought back to life and, most importantly, the White people would be driven out of the land, never to return.

Representatives from many tribes, including the Sioux, traveled to Nevada to see the Paiute Prophet. They heard his teachings with quickened hearts, and they learned from him how to perform the ritual Ghost Dance, which Wovoka said must be done by all the Indians in order to make the prophetic events a reality.

By the late fall of 1890, religious fervor was very high on the several Sioux reservations. The agents and other Whites feared that a violent outburst was imminent. At the Standing Rock Agency in North Dakota lived the man who was the greatest embodiment of Sioux resistance to White culture; Sitting Bull. He also strongly supported the Ghost Dance movement among his own people, the Hunkpapa's.

Officers of the 7th Cavalry shortly after the events at Wounded Knee.

Having decided that it was necessary to arrest the still powerful chief in the hope that this would somehow diffuse the growing defiance among the Standing Rock Sioux, the Indian agent, with the local army commander's support, decided to seize the Hunkpapa leader very early on the morning of 15 December, 1890. Shortly after a detachment of agency Indian Police escorted the protesting Sitting Bull out of his cabin, the Chief's supporters opened fire on the officers. In the first moments of the action, which left several dead on both sides, two of the policemen simply shot down the defenseless Chief.

Now, two weeks after Sitting Bull's murder, Colonel Forsyth found himself facing a group of people who were not inclined to cooperate with his demands. They were not going to give up their firearms or even admit that they had any. Had Forsyth been in a position to simply march Big Foot's people the comparatively short distance to the Pine Ridge Reservation, it seems likely that the disaster, which shortly transpired, most likely would not have happened. The Minneconjou's were, after all, entirely surrounded, out numbered and out gunned. There were also many women

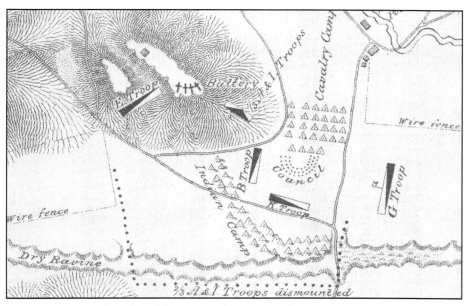

Map showing dispositions of soldiers and Indians when firing began at Wounded Knee

and children among them.

With his troops liberally mixed in among the Sioux, Forsyth sent his officers, including Captain Wallace, into the Sioux lodges to begin going through their possessions in search of arms. When Sioux women were found sitting on bundles, the officers physically picked them up and moved them to one side so the search could continue. The people looked on with growing tension. Nearby, Yellow Bird, a medicine man, harangued the warriors calling for them to resist. Some of the older men began reluctantly to come forward to surrender their weapons. Suddenly, as two soldiers grappled with a young man for possession of the Indian's rifle, it discharged. At that moment a line of warriors threw aside their blankets, which had concealed their rifles, and opened fire on a group of soldiers standing only a few yards away. In this first fusillade of bullets Captain Wallace was killed by a shot which carried away the top of his head.

A vicious struggle, interlaced with gunfire and hand-to-hand combat, then ensued. Women, children and the elderly were caught in the middle of the crossfire, some becoming casualties, while others fled to nearby ravines.

At this juncture, a battery of Hotchkiss mountain guns (small bore, rapid fire, light artillery) posted on a nearby hill opened up on Indians now firing at the hard-pressed cavalrymen from both within and near the ravines. The crashing artillery rounds, combined with rifle fire from troops on the surrounding hills, brought fearful and indiscriminate destruction to combatants and non-combatants

alike. With the stilling of the last pockets of resistance, the sanguinary struggle finally ended.

The fight at Wounded Knee left 25 soldiers and 128 Minneconjou's dead, including Big Foot and Yellow Bird, with abundant wounded on both sides. Colonel Forsyth

Remington's depiction of a Hotchkiss Gun at work at Wounded Knee.

was relieved of command by General Nelson A. Miles for placing so many of his troops in such close proximity to the Sioux, which Miles had ordered his subordinates never to do, even when Indians were friendly, and for losing control of his men.

A military Court of Inquiry determined that the soldiers, while fighting desperately, had not deliberately fired on non-combatants. The artillery battery certainly inflicted numerous casualties among women and children, but again this was not deliberate, though it made it no less unfortunate. Essentially, therefore, Forsyth had not lost control of his men. Based on Miles' standing order to avoid placing troops too close to Indians, Colonel Forsyth probably could have better positioned his men. Nevertheless, the court cleared the Colonel of any serious infraction and restored him to command.

Given the general temper of these Sioux at the time, Colonel Forsyth's orders, when implemented, practically assured the tragedy which followed.

Though a few minor incidents occurred afterward, the sad affair at Wounded Knee essentially brought down the curtain on the long, troubled era of the Indian Wars.

William B. Weir
New York.
Entered U.S.M.A. 1866.
1st Lieutenant, Ordnance.

Regular Army: *Graduated from the U.S. Military Academy and promoted to 2nd Lieutenant, 5th Artillery, on 15 June, 1870. Assigned to the Ordnance Corps, and promoted to 1st Lieutenant, on 1 November, 1874.*

On 20 October, 1879, 1st Lieutenant Weir and one of his men were killed by Ute Indians in an incident near the White River Agency, Colorado.

Melville C. Wilkinson
Born 14 November 1835.
New York.
Captain, 3rd Infantry.

Civil War Veteran, Volunteers, 1861 – 1866: Served with the 107th and 123rd New York Infantry Regiments, attaining the rank of Captain. Resigned 26 January, 1863. Served with the Veteran Reserve Corps from 13 August, 1863, attaining the rank of Captain. Honorably mustered out of the Volunteers on 30 June, 1866.

Regular Army: Commissioned 2nd Lieutenant, 42nd Infantry, on 28 July, 1866. Transferred to the 6th Infantry on 22 April, 1869. Unassigned 28 June, 1869. Assigned to the 3rd Infantry on 3 August, 1870. Promoted to 1st Lieutenant on 1 January, 1871, and to Captain, on 24 April, 1886. He served as aide to General Oliver O. Howard from April, 1871 to August, 1878.

Brevetted 1st Lieutenant and Captain respectively, on 2 March, 1867, for gallant and meritorious service at Antietam, Maryland and during the War.

Brevetted Major, on 27 February, 1890, for gallant service in action with Nez Perce Indians at the Clearwater River, Idaho, on 11 and 12 July, 1877 and at Kamiah, Idaho, on 13 July, 1877.

On 5 October, 1898, Captain Wilkinson was killed in a fight with Chippewa Indians at Bear Island on Leech Lake, Minnesota. He was the last Regular Army officer to be killed in action with Indians.

Thomas F. Wright
Born c. December 1830. Missouri.
1st Lieutenant, 12th Infantry.

Civil War Veteran, Volunteers, 1861 – 1866: Entered the Volunteers as a 1st Lieutenant and Regimental Quartermaster, 2nd California Cavalry. Honorably mustered out as Colonel, 6th California Infantry, on 16 April, 1866.

Brevetted Brigadier General of Volunteers, on 13 March, 1865, for faithful and meritorious service during the War.

__Regular Army:__ Commissioned 1st Lieutenant, 32nd Infantry, on 28 July 1866. Served as Regimental Quartermaster, 1867 – 1869. Unassigned 12 May, 1869. Assigned to the 12th Infantry on 31 January, 1870. Served as Regimental Adjutant in 1870.

      The son of General George Wright, 1st Lieutenant Wright entered the U.S. Military Academy in 1848 but left the following year without graduating.

      On 26 April, 1873, while serving in the Modoc Campaign, 1st Lieutenant Wright was killed in the Thomas-Wright Massacre by warriors led by Scarface Charley in the Lava Beds of Northern California.

George W. Yates
Born 26 February, 1843.
New York.
Captain, 7th Cavalry.

Civil War Veteran, Volunteers, 1861 – 1866: Entered the Volunteers as a Quartermaster Sergeant of the 4th Michigan Infantry. He was in action with the Army of the Potomac in the battles of First Bull Run, The Peninsula, Antietam, Fredericksburg, Chancellorsville, and Gettysburg. Honorably mustered out as a Captain, 13th Missouri Cavalry, on 11 January, 1866.

Brevetted Major of Volunteers, on 13 March, 1865, for gallant and meritorious service during the War and Lieutenant Colonel of Volunteers, same date, for conspicuous gallantry at Fredericksburg and Beverly Ford, Virginia and at Gettysburg, Pennsylvania.

Regular Army: *Commissioned 2nd Lieutenant, 2nd Cavalry, on 26 March, 1866. Served as Regimental Quartermaster in 1867. Transferred to the newly formed 7th Cavalry, and promoted to Captain, on 12 June, 1867.*

The commander of "F" Company, Captain Yates was an old friend and loyal supporter of Lieutenant Colonel G.A. Custer from the early days of the Civil War. He was at the battle of the Washita in November 1868 and was a member of both the Yellowstone and Black Hills Expeditions in 1873 and 1874.

His company was one of five composing the Custer Battalion, annihilated at the Little Big Horn on 25 June, 1876.

Footnotes

1   Major Joel Elliott—Hoig, *The Battle of the Washita*, p. 141.

2   1st Lieutenant William W. Cooke – Stewart, *Custer's Luck*, p. 341.

3 2nd Lieutenant John J. Crittenden – Thrapp, *Encyclopedia of Frontier Biography, Vol. 1* p. 346.

4   2nd Lieutenant John J. Crittenden – Graham, *The Custer Myth*, 369.

5   Major Joel Elliott – Thrapp, *Encyclopedia of Frontier Biography, Vol. 1*, p.400.

6   Capt. William J. Fetterman. D. Brown, *Fort Phil Kearny: An American Saga,* p. 150.

7   Captain Owen Hale – Beal, *I Will Fight No More Forever*, p. 215.

8   Captain Louis M. Hamilton – Heitman, *Historical Register and Dictionary of the United States Army, Vol. 1* p. 494.

9   2nd Lieutenant Benjamin H. Hodgson—Donovan, *A Terrible Glory: Custer And The Little Big Horn—The Last Great Battle of The American West*, p. 245.

10   Keenan, Jerry. *The Wagon Box Fight* Boulder, CO: Lightning Tree Press,1990, p. 22.

11 1st Lieutenant John Madagan – Thrapp, *Encyclopedia of Frontier Biography, Vol. II* p. 929.

12   Assistant Surgeon Thomas J.C. Maddox – Thrapp, *The Conquest of Apacheri*a, p. 337.

13   1st Lieutenant Edward R. Theller – Thrapp, *Encyclopedia of Frontier Biography, Vol. III* p. 1415.

14   Major Thomas T. Thornburgh—*Annual Reports of The Secretary of War, Vol. 1, November 19, 1879.*

APPENDIX A
Losses by Ranks and Branches of Service/Regiments, 1866 – 1898
(1) Brigadier General, U.S. Army

Infantry

3rd Regiment	(1) Captain	(1) 1st Lieutenant
4th Regiment	(1) Major	
5th Regiment	(1) Captain	
7th Regiment	(1) Captain	(2) 1st Lieutenants
12th Regiment	(1) 1st Lieutenant	
14th Regiment	(1) Captain	(1) 1st Lieutenant
17th Regiment	(1) 1st Lieutenant	
18th Regiment	(1) Captain	(1) 1st Lieutenant
		(1) 2nd Lieutenant
19th Regiment	(1) Lieutenant Colonel	
20th Regiment	(1) 2nd Lieutenant	
21st Regiment	(2) 1st Lieutenants	
22nd Regiment	(2) 1st Lieutenants	
27th Regiment	(1) Captain	(1) 1st Lieutenant
		(1) 2nd Lieutenant
32nd Regiment	(1) 1st Lieutenant	

Artillery

4th Regiment	(1) Captain	(3) 1st Lieutenants

Ordnance Department:
(1) 1st Lieutenant

Medical Department
(3) Assistant Surgeons

Cavalry:

1st Regiment	(1) 1st Lieutenant	(1) 2nd Lieutenant
2nd Regiment	(1) 1st Lieutenant	(2) 2nd Lieutenants
3rd Regiment	(1) Captain	(1) 1st Lieutenant
4th Regiment	(1) 1st Lieutenant	(1) 2nd Lieutenant
5th Regiment	(1) 1st Lieutenant	(1) 2nd Lieutenant
6th Regiment	(1) Captain	
7th Regiment	(1) Lieutenant Colonel	(1) Major
	(6) Captains	(6) 1st Lieutenants
		(5) 2nd Lieutenants
9th Regiment	(1) 1st Lieutenant	(2) 2nd Lieutenants
10th Regiment	(1) 2nd Lieutenant	

Summary: (1) Brigadier General; (2) Lieutenant Colonels; (2) Majors; (15) Captains; (29) 1st Lieutenants; (16) 2nd Lieutenants; (3) Assistant Surgeons.

APPENDIX B
The Army's Eight Costliest Indian Engagements After 1865: Fatalities Among Officers, Enlisted Men, Scouts and Civilians

Little Big Horn River, Montana – Sioux, Northern Cheyenne, 25 -26 June, 1876
<u>7th Cavalry</u>
15 officers   237 enlisted men   11 scouts and civilians
Total: 263

Near Fort Phil Kearny, Wyoming – Sioux, Northern Cheyenne, Arapaho, 21 December, 1866
<u>18th Infantry</u> , <u>2nd Cavalry</u>
3 officers   76 enlisted men   2 civilians   **Total: 81**

White Bird Canyon, Idaho – Nez Perce, 17 June, 1877
<u>1st Cavalry</u>
1 officer   33 enlisted men   **Total: 34**

Big Hole Basin, Montana – Nez Perce, 9 -10 August, 1877
<u>7th Infantry</u>, <u>2nd Cavalry</u>
3 officers   22 enlisted men   6 civilians   **Total: 31**

Wounded Knee Creek, South Dakota – Sioux, 29
December, 1890
<u>7th Cavalry</u>, <u>1st Artillery</u>
1 officer   24 enlisted men   **Total: 25**

Lava Beds, Northern California – Modoc, 26 April, 1873
<u>4th Artillery</u>, <u>12th Infantry</u>
5 officers   18 enlisted men   1 civilian   **Total: 24**

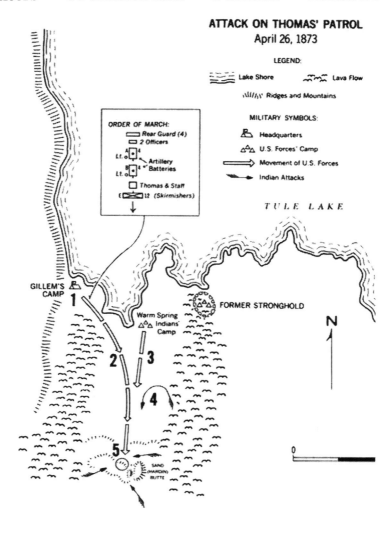

ATTACK ON THOMAS' PATROL
April 26, 1873

Bear Paw Mountains (Snake Creek), Montana – Nez
Perce, 30 September, 1877
<u>7th Cavalry</u>, <u>2nd Cavalry</u>, <u>5th Infantry</u>
2 officers   21 enlisted men   **Total: 23**

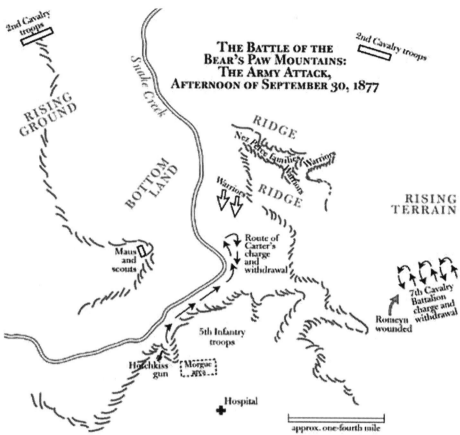

Washita River, Oklahoma – Southern Cheyenne, Arapaho,
Kiowa, Comanche, 27 November, 1868
<u>7th </u>Cavalry 2 officers   19 enlisted men   **Total: 21**

US Artillery Cap Badge, 1872

APPENDIX C
Engagements Cited in Chronological Order

1866—March 22: Cottonwood Springs (or Round Valley), Arizona. Detachment of the 14th Infantry with Apaches: 1 officer, 14th Infantry and 1 Assistant Surgeon killed.

1866--21 July: Near the Crazy Woman's Fork of the Powder River, Wyoming. Detachment of the 18th Infantry with Sioux: 1 officer, 18th Infantry, killed.

1866--6 December: Near Fort Phil Kearny, Wyoming. Detachments of the 18th Infantry and 1 company of the 2nd Cavalry with Sioux: 1 officer, 2nd Cavalry, killed.

1866--21 December: Near Fort Phil Kearny, Wyoming. Elements of 4 companies of the 18th Infantry, 1 company of the 2nd Cavalry and civilian employees with Sioux, Northern Cheyenne and Arapahos: 1 officer, 27th Infantry and 2 officers, 18th Infantry, killed. (The "Fetterman Fight," aka "Fetterman Disaster," or Massacre).

1867—c. July 2: Beaver Creek, Kansas. Detachment of the 2nd Cavalry and an Indian Scout with Sioux and Cheyenne: 1 officer, 2nd Cavalry, killed. ("The Kidder Massacre").

1867—1 August: Near Fort C.F. Smith, Montana. Detachment of the 27th Infantry and civilian employees with Sioux and Northern Cheyenne: 1 officer, 27th Infantry, killed. ("The Hayfield Fight").

1867—2 August: Near Fort Phil Kearny, Wyoming. Detachments of the 27th Infantry, and civilian employees, with Sioux: 1 officer, 27th Infantry, killed. ("The Wagon Box Fight").

1867—27 September: Infernal Caverns of the Pitt River, Northern California. 2 companies of the 1st Cavalry, 1 company of the 23rd Infantry and Warm Springs and Shoshone Indian Scouts with Pitt River and Paiute Indians: 1 officer, 1st Cavalry, killed.

1867—5 November: Near Fort Bowie, Arizona. 1 officer, 32nd Infantry, killed by Apaches.

1868—17-25 September: Arickaree Fork of the Republican River, Colorado. White scouts commanded by army officers with Southern Cheyenne and Sioux: 1 officer, 3rd Infantry, killed. (The "Beecher's Island Fight").

1868—25, 26 October: Beaver Creek and Prairie Dog Creek, Kansas. 7 companies of the 5th Cavalry and scouts with Southern Cheyenne.

1868—27 November: Washita River, Oklahoma. 11 companies of the 7th Cavalry and Osage Scouts with Southern Cheyenne, Kiowa's, Comanche's, and Arapaho's: 2 officers, 7th Cavalry, killed. ("Battle of The Washita").

1869—11 July: Summit Springs, Colorado. 7 companies of the 5th Cavalry and 3 companies of Pawnee Scouts with Cheyenne Dog Soldiers. The Cheyenne war leader, Tall Bull, was killed here, and his fierce warrior society permanently crippled as an effective fighting force.

1870—4 May: Miner's Delight, near Twin Creek, Wyoming. 1 company of the 2nd Cavalry with Northern Arapaho's: 1 officer killed.

1870—14 May: Mount Adams, Texas. Detachment of the 4th Cavalry with unidentified Indians: 1 officer killed.

1871—5 May: Whetstone Mountains, Arizona. Detachment of the 3rd Cavalry with Apaches: 1 officer killed.

1872—20 April: Near Howard Wells, Texas. Elements of the 9th Cavalry with Kiowa's: 1 officer killed.

1872—27 August: Davidson's Canyon, Arizona. 1 officer, 5th Cavalry, killed by Apaches.

1872—29 September: North Fork of the Red River (or McClellan's Creek), Texas. 5 companies of the 4th Cavalry, 1 company of the 24th Infantry, and Tonkawa Indian Scouts with Chief Push Aside's camp of Kotsoteka Comanche's.

1872—3 October: Near the Heart River Crossing, North Dakota. 1 officer, 17th Infantry, killed by Sioux.

1872—4 October—Near the Heart River Crossing, North Dakota. 1 officer, 22nd Infantry, mortally wounded by Sioux.

1872—28 December: Salt River Canyon, Arizona. 3 companies of the 5th Cavalry and Indian Scouts with Apaches.

1873—16 January: Superstition Mountains, Arizona. 6 companies of the 5th Cavalry with Apaches.

1873—11 April: Lava Beds, Northern California. 1 officer, 21st Infantry, mortally wounded by Modocs.

1873—11 April: Near Van Bremmer's Ranch in the Lava Beds, Northern California. Brigadier General Canby and Reverend Thomas killed by Modocs.

1873—26 April: Lava Beds, Northern California. Elements of 2 batteries of the 4th Artillery and 1 company of the 12th Infantry with Modocs: 3 officers, 4th Artillery and 1 officer, 12th Infantry, killed and 1 officer, 4th Artillery, mortally wounded. (The "Thomas-Wright Massacre").

1873—27 May: San Carlos Agency, Arizona. 1 officer, 5th Cavalry, killed by Apaches.

1873—4 August: Tongue River, Montana. 2 companies of the 7th Cavalry with Sioux.

1873—11 August: Yellowstone River, Montana. 8 companies of the 7th Cavalry and Indian Scouts with Sioux.

1874—9 February: Cottonwood Creek, near Laramie Peak, Wyoming. Detachments of the 2nd Cavalry and 14th Infantry, serving as a supply train guard, with Sioux and/or Northern Cheyenne: 1 officer, 14th Infantry, killed.

1876—17 June: Rosebud River, Montana. 5 companies of the 2nd Cavalry, 10 companies of the 3rd Cavalry, 2 companies of the 4th Infantry, 3 companies of the 9th Infantry, and Crow and Shoshone Scouts with Sioux and Northern Cheyenne. (The "Battle of The Rosebud").

1876—25 June: Little Big Horn River, Montana. 5 companies of the 7th Cavalry with Sioux and Northern Cheyenne: 11 officers, 7th Cavalry, 1 officer, 20th Infantry, and 1 Assistant Surgeon, killed. ("The Custer Fight", or "Custer's Last Stand").

1876—25, 26 June: Little Big Horn River, Montana. 7 companies of the 7th Cavalry and Crow and Arikara Scouts with Sioux and Northern Cheyenne: 2 officers, 7th Cavalry, killed. ("The Reno Fight," or "The Battle of Reno's Hill.").

1876—9 September: Slim Buttes, South Dakota. 5 companies of the 2nd Cavalry, 10 companies of the 3rd Cavalry, 10 companies of the 5th Cavalry, 3 companies of the 4th Infantry, 3 companies of the 9th Infantry, and 4 companies of the 14th Infantry with Sioux. The Minneconjou Chief, American Horse, was mortally wounded in this fight. (Attack on American Horse's camp by companies of General Crook's column).

1876—25 November: North Fork of the Powder River, Wyoming. 1 company of the 2nd Cavalry, 2 companies of the 3rd Cavalry, 6 companies of the 4th Cavalry, 2 companies of the 5th Cavalry, and Indian Scouts with Northern Cheyenne: 1 officer, 4th Cavalry, killed. (Attack by Colonel MacKenzie on the camps of Dull Knife and Little Wolf).

1877—8 January: Wolf Mountain, Montana. 5 companies and 2 detachments of the 5th Infantry and 2 companies of the 22nd Infantry with Sioux and Northern Cheyenne.

1877—7 May: Little Muddy Creek, Montana. 4 companies of the 2nd Cavalry, 2 companies of the 5th Infantry and 4 companies of the 22nd Infantry with Sioux. The Minneconjou Chief, Lame Deer, was killed in this fight. (Attack by Colonel Miles on Lame Deer's camp).

1877—17 June: White Bird Canyon, Idaho. 2 companies of the 1st Cavalry with Nez Perce: 1 officer, 21st Infantry, attached to the 1st Cavalry, killed. (First engagement of the Nez Perce War).

1877—3 July: Near Craig's Mountain, Idaho. Detachment of the 1st Cavalry with Nez Perce: 1 officer killed. ("The Rains' Fight").

1877—11, 12 July: South Fork of the Clearwater River, Idaho. 5 companies of the 1st Cavalry, 7 companies of the 21st Infantry and 4 batteries of the 4th Artillery with Nez Perce.

1877—13 July: Kamiah, Idaho. 4 companies of the 1st Cavalry, 7 companies of the 21st Infantry and 1 battery of the 4th Artillery with Nez Perce.

1877—9, 10 August: Big Hole Basin, Montana. Elements of 10 companies of the 7th Infantry and elements of 2 companies of the 2nd Cavalry, and civilian volunteers, with Nez Perce: 2 officers, 7th Infantry, killed and 1 officer, 7th Infantry, mortally wounded. (This battle was compared to Gettysburg by White veterans of both battles for its sheer ferocity.)

1877—30 September: Bear Paw Mountains (Snake Creek), Montana. 3 companies of the 2nd Cavalry, 3 companies of the 7th Cavalry, 5 companies and a detachment of the 5th Infantry, and Indian Scouts with Nez Perce: 2 officers, 7th Cavalry, killed.

1878—4 September: Clark's Fork, Montana. Elements of the 5th Infantry and Crow Scouts with Bannock Indians: 1 officer killed.

1878—27 September: Punished (or Famished) Woman's Fork of the Smoky Hill River, Kansas. Elements of 5 companies of the 4th Cavalry and 3 companies of the 19th Infantry with Northern Cheyenne: 1 officer, 19th Infantry, commanding the column, mortally wounded. (An incident of the "Dull Knife Episode").

1879—29 September: Milk Creek, Colorado. 1 company of the 3rd Cavalry, 2 companies of the 5th Cavalry and civilian volunteers with Ute's: 1 officer, 4th Infantry, commanding the column, killed.

1879—20 October: Near the White River, Colorado. A detachment of Indian Scouts with Ute's: 1 officer, Ordnance Corps, killed.

1880—17 January: San Mateo Mountains, New Mexico. 5 companies of the 9th Cavalry and Indian Scouts with Apaches: 1 officer, 9th Cavalry, killed. (An incident in the war with Victorio).

1881—19 August: McEver's Ranch in Guerillo Canyon, New Mexico. Elements of the 9th Cavalry, and civilian volunteers, with Apaches: 1 officer killed. (An incident of "Nana's Raid").

1881—30 August: Near Cibicu Creek, Arizona. 2 companies of the 6th Cavalry and civilian volunteers with Apaches: 1 officer killed. ("The Cibicu Affair").

1885—19 December: Little Dry Creek (or White House), New Mexico. 1 company of the 8th Cavalry and Navajo Scouts with Apaches: 1 Assistant Surgeon killed. (An incident of Ulzana's or Josanie's Raid).

1887—10 March: San Carlos Agency, Arizona. 1 officer, 10th Cavalry, mortally wounded in an assault by an Apache.

1890—15 December: Standing Rock Agency, North Dakota. A detachment of Indian Police with Hunkpapa Sioux. (Attempted arrest and subsequent murder of Chief Sitting Bull).

1890—29 December: Wounded Knee Creek, South Dakota. 8 companies of the 7th Cavalry and 1 battery of the 1st Artillery with Sioux: 1 officer, 7th Cavalry, killed. (Colonel Forsyth's fight with Big Foot's camp of Minneconjou Sioux).

1890—30 December: Near White Clay Creek (or Drexel Mission), South Dakota. 8 companies of the 7th Cavalry, 4 companies of the 9th Cavalry, 1 battery of the 1st Artillery, and Indian Scouts with Sioux: 1 officer, 7th Cavalry, mortally wounded.

1891—7 January: Near Pine Ridge Agency, South Dakota. 1 officer, 22nd Infantry, killed by a Sioux warrior.

1898—5 October: Bear Island, on Leech Lake, Minnesota. Elements of 8 companies of the 3rd Infantry with Chippewa's: 1 officer killed. ("Troubles with the Chippewa," 4-7 October, 1898).

APPENDIX D
Concerning Two Exclusions
A pair of Officers were not included in the main text.
The first is 1st Lieutenant Charles L. Hudson, 4th
Cavalry, killed by the accidental discharge of a fellow offi-
cer's weapon on 5 January, 1874. Though on active duty in
Texas fighting the Kiowa's, his death was not the result of
enemy action.

The second officer is 2nd Lieutenant Franklin Yeaton,
3rd Cavalry, severely wounded on 26 December, 1869, in
one of 1st Lt. Howard Cushing's actions with Apaches.
Yeaton lingered until 17 August, 1872, almost 32 months
after being wounded. Though ultimately a casualty of the
Indian Wars, his loss was not the immediate result of enemy
action as were the deaths of the 68 officers cited, only two of
which survived their wounds for more than two weeks.

Sources Consulted For Each Officer Listed

Lewis D. Adair: Heitman, *Register, Vol. 1; Record of
Engagements*; Ricker, Interview.

Jacob Almy: Cullam, *Biographical Register*; Heitman,
Register, Vol. 1; Thrapp, *Apacheria*; Thrapp, *Encyclopedia,
Vol. 1.*

Frederick H. Beecher: Heitman, *Register, Vol. 1*; Leckie,
Military Conquest; McHenry, *Webster's Biographies*; Powell,
List; Thrapp, *Encyclopedia, Vol. 1*; Utley, *Frontier Regulars.*

Andrew S. Bennett: M. Brown, *Nez Perce*; Greene, *Yellowstone Command*; Heitman, *Register, Vol. 1; New York Times,
13 September, 1878*; Potomac Westerners, *Western Indian
Fights*; Powell, List; Utley, *Frontier Regulars.*

Jonathan Biddle: Beal, *Fight No More*; Heitman, *Register,
Vol. 1*; Thrapp, *Encyclopedia, Vol. 1*, M. Brown, *Nez Perce.*

Horatio Bingham: D. Brown, *Fort Phil Kearny*; Heitman, *Register, Vol. 1*; Vaughn, *Indian Fights*.

James H. Bradley: Beal, *Fight No More*; D. Brown, *Fort Phil Kearny*; M. Brown, *Nez Perce*; Carroll, *Roll Call*; Gray, *Centennial Campaign*; Heitman, *Register, Vol. 1*; Michno, *Encyclopedia*; Thrapp, *Encyclopedia, Vol. 1*; Utley, *Frontier Regulars*.

Frederick H. Brown: D. Brown, *Fort Phil Kearny*; Heitman, Register, Vol. 1; O'Neal, Fighting Men.

James Calhoun: Carroll, *Roll Call*; Hammer, Biographies; Heitman, *Register, Vol. 1*; Monaghan, *Custer*; Thrapp, *Encyclopedia, Vol. 1*; Utley, *Cavalier*.

E.R.S. Canby: Heitman, *Register, Vol. 1*; Johnson, *Dictionary of American Biography, Vol. 3*; McHenry, *Webster's Biographies*; Murray, *Modocs*; Spiller, *Military Biography*; Utley, *Frontier Regulars*.

John C. Carroll: Heitman, *Register, Vol. 1*; Thrapp, *Encyclopedia, Vol. 1*.

Edward W. Casey: Cullum, *Biographical Register*: Heitman, *Register, Vol. 1*; Rodenbaugh, *Army*; Thrapp, *Encyclopedia, Vol. 1*; Utley, *Sioux Nation*.

William W. Cooke: Carroll, *Roll Call*; Hammer, *Biographies*; Heitman, *Register, Vol. 1*; Leckie, *Military Conquest*; Monaghan, *Custer*; Stewart, *Custer's Luck*.

Arthur Cranston: Cullum, *Biographical Register*; Dillon, *Burnt-Out Fires*; Heitman, *Register, Vol. 1*; Murray, *Modocs*; Thrapp, *Encyclopedia, Vol. 1*; Quinn, *Hell With The Fire Out*.

Emmet Crawford: Carroll, *Roll Call*; Heitman, Register, *Vol. 1*; O'Neal, *Fighting Men*; Powell, List; Thrapp, *Apacheria*; Thrapp, *Encyclopedia, Vol. 1.*

John J. Crittenden: Carroll, *Roll Call*; Donovan, *A Terrible Glory*; Graham, *Custer Myth*; Hammer, *Biographies*; Heitman, *Register, Vol. 1*; Thrapp, *Encyclopedia, Vol. 1.*

Eben Crosby: Heitman, *Register, Vol. 1; Record of Engagements*; Rodenbaugh, Army.

Howard B. Cushing: *Chronological List of Actions*; Heitman, *Register, Vol. 1*; O'Neal, *Fighting Men*; Thrapp, *Apacheria*; Thrapp, *Encyclopedia, Vol. 1.*

George A. Custer: Carroll, *Roll Call*; Gray, *Centennial Campaign*; Hammer, *Biographies*; Hardoff, *Hokahey!*; Heitman, *Register, Vol. 1*; McHenry, *Webster's Biographies*; Monaghan, *Custer*; Stewart, *Custer's Luck*; Warner, *Generals in Blue.*

Thomas W. Custer: Carroll, *Roll Call*; Hammer, *Biographies*; Heitman, *Register, Vol. 1*; Leckie, *Military Conquest*; Monaghan, *Custer*; O'Neal, *Fighting Men*; Thrapp, *Encyclopedia, Vol. 1*; Utley, *Cavalier.*

Napoleon H. Daniels: D. Brown, *Fort Phil Kearny*; Heitman, *Register, Vol. 1*; Johnson, *Bloody Bozeman.*

Joel H. Elliott: Barnard, *A Hoosier Quaker*; Berthrong, *Southern Cheyenne*; Greene, *Washita*; Heitman, *Register, Vol. 1*; Hoig, *Peace Chiefs*; Hoig, *Washita*; Leckie, *Military Conquest*; Nye, *Carbine and Lance*; Thrapp, *Encyclopedia, Vol. 1.*

William L. English: Beal, *Fight No More*; M. Brown, *Nez Perce*; Carroll, *Roll Call*; Heitman, *Register, Vol. 1.*

William J. Fetterman: D. Brown, *Fort Phil Kearny*; Heitman, *Register, Vol. 1*; McHenry, *Webster's Biographies*; O'Neal, *Fighting Men*; Potomac Westerners, *Western Indian Fights*; Vaughn, *Indian Fights*.

James H. French: Cullum, *Biographical Register*; Heitman, *Register, Vol. 1*; Thrapp, *Encyclopedia, Vol. 1*.

George W. Grummond: D. Brown, *Fort Phil Kearny*; Heitman, *Register, Vol. 1*; O'Neal, *Fighting Men*; Potomac Westerners, *Western Indian Fights*.

Owen Hale: Beal, *Fight No More*; M. Brown, *Nez Perce*; Carroll, *Roll Call*; Heitman, *Register, Vol. 1*; Hoig, Washita; Thrapp, *Encyclopedia, Vol. 1*.

Louis M. Hamilton: Greene, *Washita*; Heitman, *Register, Vol. 1*; Hoig, *Washita*; Leckie, *Military Conquest*; Nye, *Carbine and Lance*; Powell, *List*.

Henry M. Harrington: Carroll, *Roll Call*; Cross, Lost *Officer*; Graham, *Custer Myth*; Hammer, *Biographies*; Heitman, *Register, Vol. 1*; Stewart, *Custer's Luck*.

George M. Harris: Heitman, *Register, Vol. 1*; Murray, *Modocs*; Thrapp, *Encyclopedia, Vol. II*; Quinn, *Hell With The Fire Out*.

Edmund C. Hentig: Heitman, *Register, Vol. 1*; Lockwood, *Apache Indians*; Thrapp, *Apacheria*.

Benjamin H. Hodgson: Carroll, *Roll Call*; Donovan, *A Terrible Glory*; Hammer, *Biographies*; Heitman, *Register, Vol. 1*; Sandoz, *Little Big Horn*; Stewart, *Custer's Luck*.

Albion Howe: Dillon, *Burnt-Out Fires*; Heitman, *Register, Vol. 1;* Murray, *Modocs*; Powell, *List*; Quinn, *Hell With The Fire Out*; Utley, *Frontier Regulars*.

John C. Jenness: Heitman, *Register, Vol. 1*; Michno, *Encyclopedia*; Potomac Westerners, *Western Indian Fights*; Utley, *Frontier Regulars*.

Myles W. Keogh: Carroll, *Roll Call*; Hammer, *Biographies*; Heitman, *Register, Vol. 1*; Hoig, *Washita*; Leckie, *Military Conquest*; Luce, *Keogh*; Monaghan, *Custer*; Stewart, *Custer's Luck*.

Lyman S. Kidder: Heitman, *Register, Vol. 1*; Leckie, *Military Conquest*; Michno, *Encyclopedia*; Monaghan, *Custer*; Thrapp, *Encyclopedia, Vol. II*.

William H. Lewis: Cullum, *Biographical Register*; Heitman, *Register, Vol. 1*; Powell, List; *Record of Engagements*; Thrapp, *Encyclopedia, Vol. II*; Utley, *Frontier Regulars*.

William Logan: Beal, *Fight No More*; M. Brown, *Nez Perce*; Carroll, *Roll Call*; Heitman, *Register, Vol. 1*; Thrapp, *Encyclopedia, Vol. II*.

George E. Lord: Carroll, *Roll Call*; Graham, *Custer Myth*; Hammer, *Biographies*; Heitman, *Register, Vol. 1*.

John Madagan: Heitman, *Register, Vol. 1*; Michno, *Encyclopedia*; Thrapp, *Encyclopedia, Vol. II*.

Thomas J.C. Maddox: Heitman, *Register, Vol. 1*; Thrapp, *Apacheria*; Thrapp, *Encyclopedia, Vol. II*.

James D. Mann: Cullum, *Biographical Register*; Heitman, *Register, Vol. 1*; Utley, *Sioux Nation*; Thrapp, *Encyclopedia, Vol. II*.

Donald McIntosh: Carroll, *Roll Call*; Hammer, *Biographies*; Heitman, *Register, Vol. 1*; Philbrick, *The Last Stand*; Thrapp, *Encyclopedia, Vol. II*; Utley, *Cavalier*.

John A. McKinney: Cullum, *Biographical Register*; Heitman, *Register, Vol. 1*; Michno, *Encyclopedia*; Thrapp, *Encyclopedia, Vol. II*; Utley, *Frontier Regulars*.

James F. Millar: Heitman, *Register, Vol. 1*; Thrapp, *Encyclopedia, Vol. II*.

Seward Mott: Heitman, *Register, Vol. 1*; Thrapp, *Encyclopedia, Vol. II*.

James E. Porter: Carroll, *Roll Call*; Graham, *Custer Myth*; Hammer, *Biographies*; Heitman, *Register, Vol. 1*; Thrapp, *Encyclopedia, Vol. III*.

Sevier M. Rains: Beal, *Fight No More*; M. Brown, *Nez Perce*; Cullum, *Biographical Register*; Heitman, *Register, Vol. 1*; Thrapp, *Encyclopedia, Vol. III*.

William V.W. Reily: Carroll, *Roll Call*; Hammer, *Biographies*; Heitman, *Register, Vol. 1*.

Levi H. Robinson: Heitman, *Register, Vol. 1; Record of Engagements*; Utley, *Frontier Regulars*.

William Russell, Jr.: *Chronological List of Actions*; Heitman, *Register, Vol. 1*.

William L. Sherwood: Dillon, *Burnt-Out Fires*; Heitman, *Register, Vol. 1*; Murray, *Modocs*; Quinn, *Hell With The Fire Out*.

Algernon E. Smith: Carroll, *Roll Call*; Hammer, *Biographies*; Heitman, *Register, Vol. 1*; Hoig, *Washita*; Leckie, *Military Conquest*; Thrapp, *Encyclopedia, Vol. III*.

George W. Smith: Heitman, *Register, Vol. 1*; Powell, *List*; *Record of Engagements*; Thrapp, *Apacheria*; Thrapp, *Encyclopedia, Vol. III*.

Charles B. Stambaugh: Heitman, *Register, Vol. 1*; Powell, List; *Record of Engagements*; Michno, *Encyclopedia*.

Sigismund Sternberg: Heitman, *Register, Vol. 1*; Michno, *Encyclopedia*; Potomac Westerners, *Western Indian Fights*; Utley, *Frontier Regulars*; Vaughn, *Indian Fights*.

Reid T. Stewart: Cullum, *Biographical Register*; Heitman, *Register, Vol. 1*; Thrapp, *Apacheria*.

James G. Sturgis: Carroll, *Roll Call*; Graham, *Custer Myth*; Hammer, *Biographies*; Heitman, *Register, Vol. 1*; Thrapp, *Encyclopedia, Vol. III*.

Benjamin Tappan: Heitman, *Register, Vol. 1*; Thrapp, *Encyclopedia, Vol. III*.

Edward R. Theller: Beal, *Fight No More*; M. Brown, *Nez Perce*; Heitman, *Register, Vol. 1*; Thrapp, *Encyclopedia, Vol. III*.

Evan Thomas: Dillon, *Burnt-Out Fires*; Heitman, *Register, Vol. 1*; Murray, *Modocs*; Powell, List; *Record of Engagements*; Quinn, *Hell With The Fire Out*; Thrapp, *Encyclopedia, Vol. III*; Utley, *Frontier Regulars*.

Thomas T. Thornburgh: *Annual Reports November 19, 1879*; Cullum, *Biographical Register*; Dunn, *Massacres*; Heitman, *Register, Vol. 1*; Potomac Westerners, Western *Indian Fights*; Thrapp, *Encyclopedia, Vol. III*; Utley, *Frontier Regulars*.

Frederick R. Vincent: Heitman, *Register, Vol. 1*; Leckie, *Military Conquest*; Michno, *Encyclopedia*; Nye, *Carbine and Lance*.

George D. Wallace: Carroll, *Roll Call*; Heitman, *Register, Vol. 1*; Thrapp, *Encyclopedia, Vol. III*; Utley, *Frontier Regulars*; Utley, *Sioux Nation*.

William B. Weir: *Chronological List of Actions*; Heitman, *Register, Vol. 1*; *Record of Engagements*.

Melville C. Wilkinson: M. Brown, *Nez Perce*; Heitman, *Register, Vol. 1*; Thrapp, *Encyclopedia, Vol. III.*

Thomas F. Wright: Dillon, *Burnt-Out Fires*; Heitman, *Register, Vol. 1*; Murray, *Modocs*; Thrapp, *Encyclopedia, Vol. III*; Quinn, *Hell With The Fire Out*; Utley, *Frontier Regulars.*

George W. Yates: Carroll, *Roll Call*; Hammer, *Biographies*; Heitman, *Register, Vol. 1;* Hoig, *Washita*; Monaghan, *Custer*; Thrapp, *Encyclopedia, Vol. III*, Utley, *Cavalier.*

Bibliography

Adjutant General's Office. *Chronological List of Actions with Indians from January 15, 1837 to January 1891.* Washington, D.C., 1891.

Annual Reports of the Secretary of War, Vol.1. United States War Department. November 19, 1879 (see within the report of the General of The Army, Headquarters of the Army, Washington, DC, November 1879, page 9.

Article on the career and death of Capt. Bennett, New York Times, 13 September, 1878.

Barnard, Sandy *A Hoosier Quaker Goes to War: The Life and Death of Major Joel H. Elliott, 7th Cavalry.* Wake Forest, North Carolina, 2010.

Beal, Merrill D. *I Will Fight No More Forever: Chief Joseph and the Nez Perce War.* Seattle, Washington, 1963.

Berthrong, Donald J. *The Southern Cheyennes.* Norman, Oklahoma, 1963.

Brown, Dee *Fort Phil Kearny: An American Saga*. New York, 1962. (Republished as *The Fetterman Massacre*.)

Brown, Mark H. *The Flight of the Nez Perce: A History of the Nez Perce War*. New York, 1967.

Carroll, John M. and Price, Byron (Compilers). *Roll Call on the Little Big Horn, 28 June 1876. Vol. 3*, Source Custeriana Series. Fort Collins, Colorado, 1974.

Cross, Walt *Custer's Lost Officer: The Search for Lieutenant Henry Moore Harrington, 7th Cavalry*. Stillwater, Oklahoma, 2006.

Cullum, George W. *Biographical Register of the Officers and Graduates of the U.S. Military Academy, Vol. III Supplement*. New York, 1879.

Dillon, Richard *Burnt-Out Fires: California's Modoc Indian War*. Englewood Cliffs, New Jersey, 1973.

Donovan, James *A Terrible Glory: Custer And The Little Big Horn—The Last Great Battle of The American West*. New York, 2008.

Dunn, J.P. *Massacres in the Mountains: A History of the Indian Wars of the Far West, 1815 – 1875*. New York, 1886.

Dyer, A. B. *Handbook for Light Artillery*. New York, 1898.

Graham, Colonel William A. *The Custer Myth: A Source Book of Custeriana*. Harrisburg, Pennsylvania, 1953.

Gray, John S. *Centennial Campaign: The Sioux War of 1876*. Fort Collins, Colorado, 1976.

Greene, Jerome A. *Washita: the US Army and The Southern Cheyenne, 1867-69. Campaigns and Commanders Series, Vol. III*. Norman, Oklahoma, 2004.

Greene, Jerome A. *Yellowstone Command: Colonel Nelson A. Miles and the Great Sioux War of 1876 – 1877.* Lincoln, Nebraska, 1991.

Hammer, Kenneth (Editor) *Custer in 76: Walter Camp's Notes on the Custer Fight.* Norman, Oklahoma, 1990.

Hammer, Kenneth *Little Big Horn Biographies* (booklet) n.d.

Hardorff, Richard G. *Hokahey! A Good Day to Die! The Indian Casualties of the Custer Fight.* Frontier Military Series XVI. Spokane, Washington, 1993.

Hardy, Gordon (Senior Editor) *Above and Beyond: A History of the Medal of Honor from the Civil War to Viet Nam.* Boston, Massachusetts, 1985.

Headquarters, Military Division of the Missouri. *Record of Engagements with Hostile Indians within the Military Division of the Missouri from 1868 to 1882.* Washington, D.C., c. 1882.

Heitman, Francis B. *Historical Register and Dictionary of the United States Army, 1789 – 1903.* 2 Vols. Washington, D.C., 1903.

Hoig, Stan *The Battle of the Washita: The Sheridan-Custer Campaign of 1867 – 1869.* Garden City, New York, 1976.

Hoig, Stan *The Peace Chiefs of the Cheyennes.* Norman, Oklahoma, 1980.

Johnson, Allen (Editor) *Dictionary of American Biography, Vol. 3.* New York, 1929.

Johnson, Dorothy *The Bloody Bozeman.* New York and Toronto, 1971.

Leckie, William H. *The Military Conquest of the Southern Plains*. Norman, Oklahoma, 1963.

Lockwood, Frank C. *The Apache Indians*. Lincoln, Nebraska, 1939, 1987.

Luce, Edward S. *Keogh, Comanche and Custer*. Privately published, 1939.

McHenry, Robert (Editor) *Webster's American Military Biographies*. Springfield, Massachusetts, 1978.

Michno, Gregory F. *Encyclopedia of the Indian Wars: Western Battles and Skirmishes, 1850 – 1890*. Missoula, Montana, 2003.

Monaghan, Jay *Custer: The Life of General George Armstrong Custer*. Lincoln, Nebraska, 1971.

Murray, Keith A. *The Modocs and Their War*. Norman, Oklahoma, 1959, 1969.

Nye, Colonel Wilbur S. *Carbine and Lance: The Story of Old Fort Sill*. Norman, Oklahoma, 1937, 1962.

O'Neal, Bill *Fighting Men of the Indian Wars: A Biographical Encyclopedia*. Stillwater, Oklahoma, 1991.

Philbrick, Nathaniel *The Last Stand: Custer, Sitting Bull, and The Battle of The Little Bighorn*. New York, 2010.

Potomac Corral of the Westerners. *Great Western Indian Fights*. Lincoln, Nebraska, 1966.

Powell, Colonel William H. *List of Officers of the United States Army from 1779 to 1900*. New York, 1900.

Quinn, Arthur *Hell With The Fire Out: A History of The Modoc War*. Boston and London, 1997.

Ricker, Eli S. *Interview With Horn Chips, an Oglala Sioux.* 14 February, 1907.

Robinson III, Charles M. *A Good Year to Die: The Story of the Great Sioux War.* Norman, Oklahoma, 1995.

Rodenbaugh, Theodore F. and Haskin, William L. (Editors) *The Army of the United States.* New York, 1966.

Sandoz, Mari *The Battle of the Little Big Horn.* Philadelphia and New York, 1966.

Spiller, Roger J. and Dawson, Joseph T. (Editors) *Dictionary of American Military Biography. Vol.1.* Westport, Connecticut, 1984.

Stewart, Edgar I. *Custer's Luck.* Norman, Oklahoma, 1955.

Thrapp, Dan L. *Encyclopedia of Frontier Biography. 3 Vols.* Glendale, California, 1988.

Thrapp, Dan L. *The Conquest of Apacheria.* Norman, Oklahoma, 1967.

Utley, Robert M. *Cavalier in Buckskin: George Armstrong Custer and the Western Military Frontier.* Norman, Oklahoma, 1988.

Utley, Robert M. *Frontier Regulars: The United States Army and the Indian, 1866 – 1891.* New York, 1973.

Utley, Robert M. *The Last Days of the Sioux Nation.* New Haven, Connecticut, 1963, 1974.

Vaughn, J.W. *Indian Fights: New Facts on Seven Encounters.* Norman, Oklahoma, 1966.

Warner, Ezra *Generals in Blue.* Baton Rouge, Louisiana, 1964, 1981.

Index

Lodge Trail Ridge :43
Logan, William :57
Looking Glass :21
Lord, George E. :58
MacKenzie, Ranald S. :61
Madagan, John :58,59
Maddox, Thomas J.C. :59
Mangus :12
Mann, James D. :60
Martin, John : 28
Mathey, E. G :48
McClellan, G. B. General :17,33
McClellan Creek :61
McEvers Ranch :68
McIntosh, Donald :60,61
McKinney, John A. :61,
Medicine Lodge Treaty :12,39
Merritt, Wesley :75
Miles, Nelson A. :26,46,81
Milk Creek :74
Millar, James F. :62,72
Mimbres :44,68
Miners Delight :69
Minneconjou :52,77,79,80
Modoc :24,25,29,49,51,74
Modoc War :12,66,72,73,83
Mott, Seward :62
Mount Adams :66
Muddy Creek (Battle) :26
Nahdeizaz :63
Nana :68
Nez Perce :12,18,20,21,42,58,64,72,82
Nez Perce Campaign :17,46,77
Noch-ay-del-Klinne :49,50,78
Northern Arapaho :69
Northern Boundary Survey :14,32,54,58,63
Northern Cheyenne :12,18,23,35,36,42,54,57,61,63,64,67,70,
    74
Northern Paiute :58